This book is dedicated to my daughter,

who inspires me to be better every day.

TABLE OF CONTENTS

APPENDIX..................................... 251

Debt Relief

Chapter One
Defaulting On Your Debt

Let me be perfectly clear (especially to any attorneys who might be reading this), if you can pay back your credit card and other unsecured debts, you should. This book isn't intended to allow you to skirt your contractual obligations. That being said, many of you, for reasons outside of your control—a loss of a job or spouse, an illness in the family, etc.—will find that you can no longer make your minimum payments. Others may realize they are simply treading water by making their minimum payments and are looking for a way out. Regardless of the reason you might stop making your payments, many people find defaulting on their unsecured debt difficult from a moral or ethical perspective.

I understand, and I felt the same way too … before I learned exactly how the business of credit works.

It's Not Your Fault

I've worked in the debt relief business for almost a decade. I've worked with thousands of people and I've heard incredible stories. What, more than anything, have I learned?

It is not your fault.

The banks and credit card companies play a dirty game. They extend credit to customers who can't afford it in order to make indentured servants of us all, *and they risk almost nothing in the process.*

Let me paint a picture for you:

Somewhere in America, the Smith household carries $9,000 in credit card debt, at a rate of approximately 19%. Let's say the Smiths don't make any more charges to their card (yeah, right) and make the minimum payment of 2% of the outstanding balance until the account is paid in full. What happens next?

It will take the Smiths 81 years and 1 month to pay off the account, and they end up paying $41,796 ... for the privilege of charging the original $9,000.

The groceries, gas, clothes, and other items that were purchased on the Smith's credit card cause them to pay 464% more than someone who paid cash for those same items!

Next time you purchase a tank full of gas think about that. My tank costs about $50 to fill using my debit card. If this same tank of gas is purchased on the Smith's credit card, it will effectively cost them $232!

My goal in writing this book is to get you out of debt, restore your credit, and teach you how to use both responsibly.

Doing so, however, will start what may feel like a small war. In the course of trying to collect from you, debt collectors will come after you hard—over the phones, through the mail, and in the courts. If you don't know your rights, don't know how to protect yourself, and perhaps most importantly don't understand the *business* of debt collection ... well, good luck.

Fortunately, you don't need luck because you have this book. Not only will I show you how to fight back against unscrupulous collectors, I will show you how to:

1. Clear your debt for pennies on the dollar
2. Protect your assets
3. Restore your credit rating
4. Fight creditor harassment and lawsuits
5. And sleep well again

And as for the credit card companies, don't worry about them. Believe me, they will be just fine.

The History of Credit

Let's get one thing straight: *Credit* is not *money*.

Understanding the history of money, lending, and credit will help you get a better sense of how you ended up in the position in which you currently find yourself. To get started, let's take a quick trip back to the Dark Ages (I promise we won't stay long).

From the period between 500 A.D. and approximately 1,000 A.D., the idea of an "economy" as we know it did not exist. Money was largely nonexistent. Most people used barter to trade goods and services. The average loan was made with goods, and interest was charged with goods: if I borrowed twenty bushels of wheat, I paid back twenty bushes plus a bushel or two in interest. The barter system, and loans based on barter, helped people survive lean times and make it through the natural swings of feast and famine common in agricultural economies.

After all, sometimes the harvest doesn't come in but the kids still need to eat.

Next, certain objects such as gold coins became imbued with intrinsic value and were traded for goods and services. However, as anyone who has carried around a pocket of gold coins knows, they can be quite heavy as well as difficult to keep safe.

So strong-houses (banks) were built to store and protect these deposits of gold. In exchange for your deposit, the bank would give you a paper receipt. Soon, these receipts—being much easier to carry around—were exchanged in lieu of the gold coin backing them up in deposit.

Thus, the first paper money was created.

Then the bankers started to notice an interesting phenomenon. Given their daily deposits and withdrawals, there was always a certain amount of gold on hand in deposits. Since the receipts for these deposits were as good as money (and indeed functioned as our modern currency does), the bankers started issuing more deposit receipts than they actually had gold in deposit. Why?

Because the bankers knew that by issuing extra deposit receipts, there wouldn't be enough gold in deposit if everyone were to cash their receipts at the same time. However, the bankers also knew they could always count on a certain percentage of gold to remain in deposit and therefore banks could *literally print money for themselves*, based upon other peoples' gold, by simply creating these additional fiat receipts!

This original deception by bankers was the genesis for the credit and fractional reserve system that we have today.

Ethical Lending

I have pretty strong feelings about lending. In simple terms, I think some lending is, for want of a better term, *good*, and some lending is, well, considerably less than good. To illustrate the point, let's take a quick look at a lending practice I think makes sense.

Say I find myself in a financial bind and could really use a loan. I turn to you for help. We draw up a contract. You lend me $1,000, and I promise to pay the money back with interest.

Why should I pay interest? Because, when you lend me money, you transfer ownership of that money to me. I can use it for whatever purpose I decide and you no longer have that luxury. You can't invest it, you can't put it in a savings account. In effect, you lose the opportunity to benefit from the money you lend me. That lost benefit is considered an opportunity cost. To compensate you for the lost opportunity, I agree to pay interest on the money you lend.

It's only fair.

So we both decide 5% is a reasonable interest rate. That's not usurious, or excessive. Each state has usury laws intended to protect consumers from usurious lending practices (so-called Loan Shark Laws), and each state specifies what it considers to be excessive interest rates and terms.

Oops. Except Delaware and South Dakota—they don't have usury laws on the books. As a result it should come as no surprise that Delaware, a state where setting up a company is incredibly easy, is also the "credit card capital" of the United States. Incorporate a credit card company in Delaware or South Dakota and you don't have to worry about following usury laws. You can charge what you want. (FYI, it might *look* like these states have usury limits in place, but banks easily get around them.)

So let's get back to the money you agree to lend me. We decide 5% is a fair interest rate, and we also create a payment schedule so we both know what's expected.

Simple, right? We reach a fair agreement, you help me out, and I feel obligated to pay back the loan with interest. I not only want to return what is yours (the $1,000 principal), but also compensate you for your opportunity cost (the 5% interest). I feel a moral obligation to make good on my debt to you and will do everything I possibly can to make sure I pay you back.

This view of lending is how most people view credit card debt, *but they're dead wrong*.

The Credit Scam

In order to determine whether to extend you credit, a credit card company checks out your credit report and current income to create a risk profile for you. With millions of historical data points at their disposal, they can predict with statistical certainty whether you are worth the gamble of extending credit.

And that's fine. Credit card companies are smart to determine how much risk they face if they approve your credit card application, and how high a credit limit they should extend. All of this makes perfect sense and is absolutely reasonable if credit card companies actually lent money—but they don't.

They extend *credit*.

See if you can follow this shell game.

The moment you sign a credit card application, that piece of paper is magically transformed from a worthless piece of paper into a negotiable debt instrument the bank can use. You sign a contract, and that contract instantly has value for the bank based upon the statistical similarity you have to the millions of people like you (assuming they decide to extend you credit).

The contract's value was not created from the exchange of money or goods or services, or in fact from anything other than your signature on a piece of paper. In fact, if you were to get a peek at the credit card company's underlying accounting ledgers you would see your credit account is actually recorded as an *asset* rather than a *liability*.

And the rabbit hole goes even deeper.

After monetizing your signature, the credit card company then lends the value you created back to you in the form of credit and presto—*you have effectively just funded your own credit card account!* If you have been looking for one of the eggs that hatched the chicken that created the recent financial crisis, here it is.

But we're not done yet! Now I want you to pay close attention. Nothing up my sleeves … ready …

The payments you make to the credit card companies are with *real money*.

Let me say that again in case you missed it: *you pay your credit card bill with REAL MONEY!*

Up until you start making payments, there hasn't been any real money used in this little shell game. At this point you should be thinking, "Are you $%&*! kidding me!!!" And to that I can only say, "I wish I was."

Credit card companies lend you *nothing*, charge you interest on *nothing*, and then take *real* money from you in the form of payments. So if you default, the credit card companies are in most cases out—say it with me—nothing. Now, of course the credit card companies did have to "pay" for those goods and services you charged on the card, but remember, that credit was created out of your signature in the first place. Only if you default on the card does your balance become a liability. But, on average, most people end up paying multiple times what they borrow (as in the Smith family example above), so the card companies aren't really taking a loss at all. Add to this the tax write-offs, insurance, and the money they get from selling your account to 3rd party debt collectors, and they are doing just fine.

In short, credit card companies have it all figured out. They have rigged the system so that—like Vegas—the house always wins. The playing field is steeply slanted in their favor by their ability to create value out of your signature, use that value to fund your account, charge interest on that value you provide, and get paid back in real dollars.

Fractional Reserve Lending

Remember those early bankers who wrote extra receipts for gold deposits and effectively printed money? Didn't that sound at least devious if not downright immoral and unlawful? If you or I were to print money we'd be locked up, guaranteed!

Not only does this practice continue today, it is the very basis of our banks' lending structures. Rather than calling it what it is—a license to print money based on using other peoples' deposits— today we call it *Fractional Reserve Lending*. The name may have changed, but the practice remains exactly the same.

Say you want to start a bank. Federal and state guidelines require you to have a certain amount of money in "reserves". In 2011, for Net Transaction Accounts these reserves are:

Reservable Liability	Reserve Requirement
$0 to reserve requirement exemption amount ($10.7 million)	0 percent of amount
Over reserve requirement exemption amount ($10.7 million) and up to low reserve tranche ($58.8 million)	3 percent of amount

Over low reserve tranche ($58.8 million)	$1,443,000 plus 10 percent of amount over $58.8 million

Source: www.federalregister.gov

Through the principle of fractional reserve lending, a bank can lend a multiple of the money it actually has in reserve. Therefore, if a bank has $58.8 million in cash reserves (the low reserve trench limit in the table above), it can actually make $1.96 billion in loans AND charge interest on that money!

As an individual you can't do that. You can't lend money you don't have and charge interest on it. And furthermore, all of this is hugely inflationary.

As of March 2009, U.S. revolving consumer debt, made up almost entirely of credit card debt, stood at about $950 billion.[1] Ask any economist and they will tell you that expanding the money supply in this fashion is hugely inflationary and decreases the purchasing power of *real* money, yours and mine.

The Credit Industry

Now let's look at today's credit card industry.

The number keeps growing, but as of November 2010 Americans owed about $836 billion in credit card debt. The average American

---

[1] U.S. Congress' Joint Economic Committee, "Vicious Cycle: How Unfair Credit Card Company Practices Are Squeezing Consumers and Undermining the Recovery," May 2009

household had $15,788 in credit card debt at an average interest rate of 14.48%.[2]

And the credit card companies have done really well, despite the recession. Credit card companies made about $18.5 billion in profits in 2010.[3]

One of the ways they made those profits is by taking advantage of, well, all of us. The terms and conditions you originally agree to are often quickly changed, and always in the bank's favor. Think about a recent credit card bill and the charges you see listed. You might have paid a late payment fee, a cash advance fee, a balance transfer fee, and an "over maximum credit limit" fee.

Sadly, credit card companies were at one time regulated to limit unfair practices. Up to 1978, most states had usury laws on the books ensuring that interest rates and fees were capped. In most cases, interest rates could not exceed 18%.

Not anymore.

In 1978, the Supreme Court decided that when a national bank located in one state had credit card customers residing in a different state, the maximum interest rate allowed and amount of other fees was determined by the laws of the bank's *home* state, regardless of where its customers might reside.

---

[2] http://www.creditcards.com/credit-card-news/credit-card-industry-facts-personal-debt-statistics-1276.php
[3] R.K. Hammer Investment Bankers press release 1.3.2011

What did the banks do? Packed up and moved to Delaware and South Dakota, states with no usury laws and no limits on credit card interest rates.

And you and I are the lucky recipients of that particular ruling.

In May of 2009 Congress passed the CARD Act that reins in some of the most offensive credit card practices such as double-cycle billing, universal default clauses, and over-limit fees, but the credit card industry is always one step ahead. They have already come up with new ways to charge additional fees such as an annual fee for not charging *enough* on our cards, or even a fee for paying off your balance every month!

Well, that's it for your crash course in the business of banks and credit. I hope you can see now that your credit card balance is unlike any loan you might have received from a friend or family member. The banks are playing a dirty game and the odds are stacked against you.

Now, let's see what you can do to even the odds a little.

Chapter Two
Traditional Debt Relief Strategies

Years ago, in a world far, far away, I was a second-year medical school student with a full scholarship.

And I hated it.

Maybe "hate" is a strong word. But I soon realized I didn't love medicine enough to make it my career. I believe you have to love what you do to do it well, and I just didn't love the idea of practicing medicine, much less spending years in medical school and residency.

So what did I do?

Since I was a child I had always wanted to be an inventor. So I left medical school, bought all the books I could find on inventing, and I studied and worked and dreamed big, all in a quest to invent the next best thing.

The problem was, I knew a lot about inventing, but almost nothing about running a business.

I had formed a sole proprietorship instead of a corporation (strike one). I racked up almost $100,000 in debt (strike two). At the time, I wondered how a self-employed (unemployed) guy in his twenties could get that much credit, but I put those concerns aside and plowed ahead.

Finally I managed to license one of my inventions, but the royalties weren't enough to turn the tide (strike three). I simply couldn't service my debt any longer and the house of (credit) cards collapsed.

So, using the Internet, I started researching my options.

I checked out the possibility of consolidation, negotiation, and settlement, even bankruptcy. In the process, I ran into a company promising a unique form of debt relief that was a bit less mainstream. I figured it was worth a shot.

While the company (which shall remain nameless) didn't deliver as promised, it did provide me with a running start. Through trial, error, and a few hard knocks, I learned a lot about my rights as a consumer, as well as about the debt collection business and court procedure. At the end of the day, I was able to effectively walk away from my debt for about 4 cents on the dollar AND repair my credit.

My own experiences—and what I now know after spending almost a decade in the debt relief and credit repair industry—serves as the basis for this book. Though I obviously recommend the strategies contained herein, it is certainly not the only way forward. Ultimately, my goal is to help you make an informed decision about what is best for *you* and *your* situation. Therefore, it is important that you understand the pros and cons of the other traditional debt relief strategies available.

Debt Consolidation

Debt consolidation programs come in two flavors:

A secured loan, (like a home equity or home improvement loan) taken out to pay off your smaller accounts, and

An unsecured loan, such as a signature loan from a bank, or a new credit card.

When you consolidate debts, you enjoy the convenience of paying a single creditor under new terms. When shopping for a consolidation loan, the new terms should ideally be better than the terms of the accounts you are consolidating. With the right loan, the savings can be significant.

For example, say you owe $20,000 on 2 credit cards, your average interest rate is 22%, and your minimum monthly payments total $700. If you were to continue making minimum payments and not make any more charges, it would take you 41 months to pay off those cards and cost $28,700. If you managed to qualify for a consolidation loan for $20,000 at an interest rate of 12%, and managed to keep your minimum payments of $700 per month, you would pay the loan off in 34 months and save almost $5,000! Even if you bumped your payments down to $500 per month, you would still save $2,700 when compared to your 22% rate.

So let's take a closer look at your options, starting with a secured home equity loan. The great thing about home equity loans is that the rates are excellent when compared to your credit cards. The disadvantage is that not only do you need to own a home, you must have more than 20% equity in that home to qualify. Another way to say this is that you can only borrow up to 80% of your home's value, including your mortgage. Say your home was worth $100K and you have paid your mortgage down to $60K. That means you have 40% equity in your home and would probably qualify for a $20K loan.

Though paying off higher interest rate cards with a lower interest rate home equity loan may seem like a good idea at first, there are a few caveats to consider. First, why do you think you are able to qualify for a lower rate with a home equity loan? Because credit cards are *unsecured* debt and a home equity loan is a *secured* debt.

What's the difference? Unsecured debt is debt without collateral: you qualified for your credit card based on your credit history and your signature alone. Secured debt is based on collateral: if you borrow money to buy a car, the car is the collateral and the lender will come after the car if you default on the loan. The same applies with a home equity loan. Unsecured debt is difficult to collect on since there is no collateral securing the debt. This is why credit cards and unsecured debt carry higher interest rates and why secured loans, in general, carry lower interest rates.

Pay off credit cards with a home equity loan, and you just transformed unsecured debt into secured debt and put your home within reach of your creditors. And since most people who get a home equity loan find themselves in the same amount of credit card debt 3-5 years later, those who aren't careful might find themselves in the same position in the near future without that equity to tap in their home.

The second kind of debt consolidation loans are offered by credit card companies and banks with introductory, low-interest rates. These rates are very attractive for good reason: they are counting on the fact that you won't pay off your debt during the introductory period. Whatever principal balance remains after the introductory period expires is subject to the much higher, non-introductory rate. Make sure you are aware of this rate before you accept any introductory offer.

The beauty of these types of offers is that they are offering money at rates much lower than usual, even when compared to secured debt rates. I have a friend who actually has great credit, accepts these low introductory-rate offers, and then invests the money at a higher rate of return.

How can banks lend at such low introductory rates? Because the non-introductory rate is high enough to make up the difference when the introductory rate expires.

You might be thinking, "I get introductory offers in the mail all the time. Why can't I just keep transferring my balance to a new card with a new introductory rate?" You can, but eventually you will stop receiving those offers in the mail. Though you can save some money in lower interest rates doing the credit card shuffle, it WILL negatively impact your credit score, and eventually you will no longer qualify for those introductory rates. When this happens, you might find yourself with a higher interest rate card than when you started, without the luxury of another introductory rate to switch to. However, all the interest you saved in the interim might just make it worthwhile.

Another option to consider instead of a consolidation loan is a debt waterfall program. The reasoning behind these programs is simple: make your minimum payments on all accounts and take any remaining money you have each month to pay down your account with the highest interest rate. Interest is what makes debt so profitable for banks and expensive for us, the consumer. Interest charged on your accounts reduces your available monthly cash to spend. Therefore, if you begin to eliminate higher interest debt first, you have more money available to pay off your other debt faster. As you go through this process, you accelerate the rate at which you are paying off the same amount of debt, making you debt-free faster. In order to leverage a debt waterfall program, you have to be financially capable of paying *more* than your minimum monthly payments. If not, a debt waterfall program is out of reach for you.

The pros and cons of debt consolidation are:

Pro: Lower interest rates

Pro: One check to write each month

Pro: Maintain a positive credit rating

Con: Secured loans transform unsecured debt into secured debt

Con: Can create the false sense that all is okay with your finances, and may encourage additional spending

Con: The credit card shuffle (switching from one introductory rate to another) may negatively impact your credit score

Debt Negotiation and Settlement Companies

Most of the ads you see for debt relief are from debt negotiation and settlement companies. These companies negotiate on your behalf with your creditors in order to reach settlement agreements acceptable to all parties. The clear benefit of working with a debt negotiation and settlement company is that you are working with a trained professional. Moreover, the larger negotiation and settlement companies can actually negotiate better deals for their clients due to the amount of debt they control among various creditors.

Here are some factors to consider when shopping for a negotiation and settlement company:

The company you choose should be a member of either TASC (The Association of Settlement Companies) or USOBA (United States Organization for Bankruptcy Alternatives).

It should be accredited. Check each company you consider at tascsite.org or usoba.org. While just being a member isn't necessarily good enough, accreditation means a company is part of the elite for that trade association.

Make sure you understand all the fees associated with the program. Under existing UDMSA (Uniform Debt-Management Services Act) legislation, companies are generally allowed to charge up to 17% of your debt. You may also be liable for taxes on the difference between what you owe and the amount for which they settle.

Remember, even though you are paying the negotiation and settlement company each month, YOU are still liable for the debt, and collection efforts will still proceed against YOU until a settlement agreement is reached. For a referral to our accredited negotiation and settlement partner, visit DebtClear.com.

DIY Debt Settlement

According to Generally Accepted Accounting Principles (GAAP), if a consumer has not made a payment on a debt for six months (technically 180 days), the original creditor generally records the debt as a loss, gets a tax deduction, collects any insurance money they have in place against bad debts, and may sell your account to a debt-buyer.

Before the 180 days is up, the original creditor will probably offer you a settlement. Should you take it? I can't answer that question for you. Just keep in mind the credit card company's settlement offer may be as high as 70%-80% of the original debt; if they are negotiating near the end of the six-month period, they may go as low as 40% in some cases, but quite frankly, that kind of offer is unlikely. Credit card companies can discharge the debt and get a 20-30% tax write-off, and may receive insurance payments and be able to sell it for 8-12 cents on the dollar. As a result, they won't offer to settle for less than what they could otherwise receive. If you want to pay as little as possible to settle the debt, you stand a much better chance dealing with a debt-buyer, who has a lot less invested in the account.

Why would the credit card company (original creditor) decide to sell your account rather than continuing to try to collect? Currently, credit card companies are discharging over 100,000 accounts a month each, and that number continues to grow. Some individual credit card companies discharge over 1,000,000 accounts each month!

That's just too many accounts for a credit card company to deal with—they are in the lending business, not the debt collection business. And the playing field is tilted in the credit card company's favor, anyway. They figure they have probably already made a nice return on those accounts already, so they sell the debt to a debt collector and call it quits.

A debt collector will purchase your debt for, at most, 15 cents on the dollar from the original creditor. They might try to collect for 6 months or a year. If they sell it to another debt collector, it will likely be for around 5 cents on the dollar. The longer your debt has been around, the less it is worth and the less they will settle for.

(If you want to try settling your accounts on your own, refer to the tutorial on debt settlement in the Roadmap section of this book, or at DebtClear.com.)

In closing, here are the pros and cons of debt negotiation and settlement to consider:

Pro: Accredited settlement companies leverage professionals and large portfolios to work for you, giving you a much stronger negotiating position.

Pro: You'll likely pay back less than what you owe and you'll do it on a budget that you control.

Pro: Once a settlement has been reached, you are done!

Pro: You can usually have your credit report updated to "paid as agreed."

Con: Collections efforts WILL continue. You owe the debt, and collectors will still try to get you to pay them directly.

Con: Your credit score will be negatively impacted. Getting new credit will be really tough and expensive while in a program.

Con: You may have to pay taxes on the difference between what you owe and what you settle for.

Credit Counseling

If you have just gotten a little behind on your debts and need some help with your monthly payments and interest rates, credit counseling may be right for you. It is important to note that you will be paying back 100% of your debt in a Consumer Credit Counseling Service (CCCS) program. Debt relief comes in the form of reduced interest rates and an accelerated pay-off period, not principal reduction.

Many for profit and non-profit CCCS agencies have pre-negotiated terms with credit card issuers. These terms allow for *interest rate reductions* as long as you maintain your payment schedule.

Other significant benefits of CCCS enrollment are that collection activities cease and your credit score isn't negatively impacted, though enrollment in a CCCS is visible on your credit report and may impact your credit worthiness with some creditors. To determine whether you are a good candidate for CCCS, ask yourself:

- Can I afford 80-90% of your current minimum monthly payments?
- Are my interest rates higher than average?
- Do I feel confident I can stick to the scheduled payment plan for an extended period of five years or more?

A final benefit of using a CCCS is that they do it all for you. Just send them a check every month and they handle the rest. Here are the pros and cons to consider:

Pro: 10-20% reduction in your minimum monthly payments.

Pro: You reduce your effective pay-off amount and shorten your pay-off period.

Pro: Collection activities, if started, should stop.

Pro: It doesn't affect your credit score.

Pro: You write a single check each month.

Con: CCCS or a Debt Management Plan (DMP) is noted on your credit report. If you need new credit, lenders are less likely to extend it to you while you are in a DMP.

Con: You still pay back 100% of your debts, albeit at lower interest rates, over a period of 5 or more years.

Con: Some forms of debt won't be included in a CCCS program (some medical debt, for example).

For a referral to an accredited credit counseling program you can trust, visit DebtClear.com.

Bankruptcy

There are two types of personal bankruptcy: Chapter 7 and Chapter 13. Chapter 7, also referred to as a liquidation bankruptcy, erases all debts that are legally capable of discharge. Chapter 13 bankruptcy reorganizes debt into a repayment plan over a period of three to five years.

In order to qualify for Chapter 7, the filer's income must fall below the median income of their state. If the filer's income is over their state's median, then they must take a "means test" to establish their eligibility. The means test assesses the filer's ability to pay back their creditors by looking at debt and income over the previous six months. If there is any income remaining each month to pay creditors, they will fail the means test and have to file Chapter 13.

In a Chapter 7, any assets you have over an allowed value will be sold (liquidated) to at least partially satisfy creditors, and the rest of your qualifying debt will be forgiven. The process takes from four to six months, and you will be required to complete a credit counseling program with a government-approved agency. You will not qualify for a Chapter 7 bankruptcy if you have filed another bankruptcy within the past six to eight years.

With Chapter 13 filings, instead of selling your assets to pay creditors, you get to keep those assets, but agree to pay some or all of what you owe to your creditors over a three to five year period. You will be required to enter credit counseling from an approved agency. Then you'll start making payments. Priority debts, like back child support and tax obligations, must be paid off in full and are not included in the restructuring plan. Then you will be required to make normal payment on secured debts, like home loans and auto loans once you reaffirm[4] the debt. Money left over will go towards repaying unsecured debt like credit cards. When the repayment period is over, any remaining balance you owe on unsecured debts will be eliminated.

Bankruptcy can:

- **Eliminate credit card debt, personal loans, and unsecured debt.** Filing bankruptcy wipes out unsecured debt, since no collateral was pledged.

- **End harassment from creditors and collection agencies.** Not only will you end phone calls and letters, but you might also stave off repossession or foreclosure.

---

[4] A process where the borrower agrees to pay the existing note off in full under the terms originally signed.

Bankruptcy cannot:

- **Prevent repossession.** Bankruptcy eliminates unsecured debts, but does not remove secured loans. If you secure a loan with property, bankruptcy eliminates the loan but may still allow the lender to repossess the property securing the loan.

- **Wipe out child support and alimony.** Even if you file for Chapter 7, these debts are considered priority debts and must be paid.

- **Eliminate outstanding student loans.** While it is possible you can show that repaying a student loan causes "undue hardship," proving undue hardship is incredibly difficult.

- **Wipe out tax debt.**[5]

- **Wipe out judgments, fines, penalties, or traffic tickets.**

Perhaps the largest *disadvantage* to bankruptcy is its impact on your credit rating. Chapter 7 stays on your credit report for 10 years, Chapter 13 for 7 years. A bankruptcy can make it nearly impossible to get a mortgage for up to five years. It will make it harder to buy a car, get life insurance, qualify for other forms of credit, and sometimes even to land a job. A bankruptcy is the single *worst* thing you can have on your credit report. Finally, even the simplest of bankruptcies will cost you around $2,000. If you had that kind of money lying around, I bet you would still be making your minimum payments.

Here's the bottom line: if you qualify for Chapter 7, it is a viable debt relief option despite its damage to your credit report. If you only qualify for Chapter 13, I recommend looking into other options

---

[5] You can discharge tax debt in Chapter 7 in some rare cases.

such as debt settlement or this program. By including all of your debts in a Chapter 13, you are giving up your rights to dispute any of that debt down the road, which—as you will learn shortly—can be a powerful debt relief strategy.

So, let's review the pros and cons of bankruptcy.

Pro: Collection activities stop. The bankruptcy court will issue an automatic stay halting collection activities and any pending lawsuits.

Pro: If you qualify for Chapter 7 you can get rid of most of your debts and get on with your life in a matter of months.

Pro: Chapter 13 allows you to keep your assets and potentially eliminate unsecured debt.

Con: Bankruptcy is a nuclear bomb to your credit score and credit report. The "fallout" sticks around for 7 – 10 years and makes borrowing much more costly.

Con: Chapter 13 is the least favorable and most common form of bankruptcy filing. You'll pay back a good portion of what you owe and still have "bombed" credit to boot. This is an expensive proposition in the short and long-term.

Con: You affirm your debt obligations in Chapter 13, making it more difficult to employ other debt relief tactics down the road.

To find out if bankruptcy might be right for you, contact a bankruptcy attorney in your area or visit DebtClear.com for a referral.

Chapter Three
The Business of Debt Collection

Debt collection is a business just like any other. Debt collectors try to make the most profit they can given their limited time and resources.

I like to use the analogy of an apple tree. Pretend you are the apple and the debt collection companies are the harvesters. Have you ever seen apples harvested from a commercial orchard? First they bring in huge tree shakers and shake the tree, hard and fast. Shaking brings down most of the fruit. To get some of what remains, the orchard might bring in people to pick the low-hanging fruit.

But the high-hanging fruit that hung on tightly enough to withstand the initial shaking, and is out of reach of the pickers, often gets left on the tree.

Why?

The tough, high-hanging fruit is too difficult and expensive to collect.

The costs associated with paying someone to climb up into the upper branches—the time, liability, manpower—are more than the apple can be sold for. So the orchard "writes off" that fruit and focuses on the easy fruit to pick.

Just like apple farms are in the business of making money, debt collection companies are too. If you are high-hanging fruit—if you are too difficult or expensive to collect on—they will just leave you there and move on to the next tree. After all, there's plenty of low-hanging fruit on the next tree, so why waste time on you?

The goal of this program is to teach you how to become the tough, high-hanging fruit. To understand how to get there, you will first need to understand who is trying to pluck you from the tree.

Original Creditors

The original creditor is the credit card company where you opened an account. (In fact, an original creditor is any lender that initially gave you a loan, but for the purposes of this discussion we'll focus on credit card companies as original creditors.)

You open an account and everything is fine until you fail to make a payment. What happens first? For the first month or two you will see late fees and penalties, and your interest rate is likely to jump to 29% or higher! This is good news for the credit card company. They actually like it when you fall behind because they make more money (in 2009 credit card companies made about $20.5 billion in penalty fees alone).[6]

However, the credit card companies only profit from your delinquency if you catch up on your payments and pay the penalties and higher interest rate they are now charging on your card. After 2-3 months of non-payment, you are likely to receive a (somewhat) friendly call from your credit card company's call

---

[6] New York Times, September 2009

center. You will be reminded that the call may be recorded for "training purposes."

Then they'll ask about the payment you missed. They may ask why you didn't make the payment on time. They may ask other questions. But mainly they will attempt to get you to make the payment, preferably over the phone, immediately. Short of that, they hope to gather information that can be used against you if you continue to stay in default on the account.

You could make the payment over the phone, but that puts an end to our story. Let's assume you don't. What happens next?

Of course they keep calling, and calling. You'll also get notices in the mail. Like the phone calls, the notices will start out friendly, using language like, "Perhaps your payment has already been mailed. If so, thanks!" Then the language will get more serious, and thinly veiled threats will become less veiled and a lot more open. The goal, of course, is to scare and intimidate you into getting your account out of default.

Credit card companies will generally try to collect on an account in default for six months, after which they will charge it off their books as bad debt. The credit card company reports the debt as a loss on their financial reports, gets a tax write-off, and will either sell or assign your debt to a debt collector (we'll talk about debt collectors in the next chapter).

Around month three or four, the credit card company may offer you a settlement. Every company has different practices, but, as an example, your credit card issuer may offer to settle the account for 60% of the balance. If you pay them $6,000, they will wipe out your $10,000 debt. They will also report the settlement to the credit bureaus as "settled for less than full amount" and are required to file a 1099 form with the IRS showing you had additional "income" that tax year of $4,000.[7]

Why might the credit card company be willing to settle before the six-month charge-off date? Remember, they probably carry insurance on the debt, they can take a tax write-off, and they can sell the debt to a collection agency. Say the write-off is worth 20% of the amount of the debt and they will receive a 10% insurance settlement, plus they can sell the debt to a debt collector for 10% of its value. Their exposure has been cut to 60% of the value of the total debt. If they can settle with you for 40%, they are just breaking even.

If you have the money to settle your debts with the original creditor, making an offer of 40% or more after not paying for about five months isn't a bad strategy. You can experience sizable debt relief and the debt "dies on the vine." You might also be able to have your credit report updated to "paid as agreed" as part of the settlement (much better than "settled for less than full amount") and have any negative credit entries removed. (You can try negotiating and settling your debts yourself after reading our tutorial on debt settlement in the Roadmap section of this book. Alternatively, you can find a referral for a trusted and accredited professional at DebtClear.com.)

---

[7] Only about 15-20% of those settling accounts actually receive a 1099 for the difference.

Note that some original creditors may choose to assign or sell your debt to a collection company earlier than six months after non-payment. Keep that fact in mind, not only if you are considering settling with the original creditor, but also because your rights differ depending on whether you're being contacted by an original creditor or a debt collector (more on this in later sections).

Should I Ask the Original Creditor for Help?

Say you just lost your job. You haven't fallen behind on your payments yet, but you're scared you will be forced to do so very soon. You're trying to be proactive, do the right thing, and you ask your credit card company, "Can we work out some type of deal until I get back on my feet?"[8]

The answer will be an emphatic "No."

The credit card company doesn't care about you. It doesn't care about your problems. Credit card companies only care about money. If you are current on your payments, they are making money. If you are 1-2 months behind, they are still making money (at least on paper) in late payments and interest hikes. It is only once it looks like you won't pay them, ever, that they will start to deal.

Therefore, the only way to get an original creditor's attention is to stop paying your bill for a few months.

---

[8] Contacting your creditor for help often "flags" your account and they will begin tracking your purchases and usage more closely.

Initially they will threaten you, but won't offer any kind of settlement. Only after a few months pass, and the six-month charge-off date looms on the horizon, will they be willing to settle. In fact, the closer you are to the six-month charge-off period, the more likely they will be to deal and the better the deal will be.

But they will never work with you when you're current on your payments. It just won't happen, so don't even bother trying.

Debt Collectors

Debt collectors are not original creditors: they don't make loans or issue credit cards, they just collect debts. In some cases they work on a fee or contingency basis. In other cases they purchase bad debt from a credit card company for pennies on the dollar and then attempt to collect the debt as an independent 3rd party.[9]

For example, say you have a $10,000 balance on a credit card. You stop making payments and after six months the credit card company writes the account off as bad debt. At this point the original creditor will either assign or sell the debt.

If they assign the debt, then the original creditor still owns the account, but they contract with an outside firm to collect on it. Typically assignee debt collectors are paid on a percentage basis of what they can recover.

---

[9] In general, if you are being contacted within the first year of being in default you are being contacted by a contingency collector to whom the debt has been assigned. Once you get outside that timeframe, your account has generally been bought by a third-party debt-buyer.

If your debt is sold, a collection company actually buys your debt from the original creditor for somewhere around ten cents on the dollar. The collection company now owns the debt and the original creditor has given up all rights, title, and interest. This scenario is not only the most common, but is also better for you.

Why?

Allow me to answer that question with a question. If you had a credit card through XYZ Bank and they sold it to ABC Collection Company, do you have an agreement with ABC Collection Company? No, you don't. You had an agreement with XYZ bank. For now, suffice to say it is a legal distinction that can make a big difference, as you will soon learn.

Now the new owner, ABC Collection Company, has the right to collect on your debt. In fact, many will add on penalties and interest in hopes of getting even more money, and short of that, setting a higher starting point for haggling with scared, intimidated, and uninformed consumers.

When the original creditor first offers your account for sale, debt collectors are willing to pay the most for it. In general, your credit card account might fetch 8 – 12% of its value the first time it is sold. The debt collector who purchases your account may work it hard for three to six months, but if they aren't successful they will likely cut their losses and sell your account to someone else—this time for maybe 5 – 8%.

The pattern continues and, years later, a debt collector might pay as little as .25% for your account (especially if the statute of limitations on collecting that debt is near). Over time your account could be bought and sold several times.

Because they have invested the most in your account, the initial debt-buyer of your account will work the hardest to collect on it. They have the most to lose if they fail. After all, if a debt collector buys a $10,000 debt for $1,000 and collects the full amount, they have just made a 1,000% return on their investment!

As you will learn in the next chapter, what debt collectors do and what they are *allowed* to do under Federal law are two entirely different things. Unfortunately, violating your rights is simply good business and extremely effective. Not knowing your rights is like swimming in murky waters with sharks!

Whether your debt is sold or assigned, the debt collector is governed by the Fair Debt Collections Practices Act (FDCPA), a set of federal rules regulating the debt collection industry. In short, the FDCPA is like a bill of consumer rights designed to protect you from abuse, intimidation and fraud in the debt collection industry.

For example, the FDCPA requires any debt collector to send what is called a dunning letter within five days of contacting you. Usually the first contact *is* the dunning letter, but, if a debt collector calls, they have five days to send a dunning letter (they can also make the same disclosures verbally by phone). While the language contained in dunning letters may vary, in basic terms a dunning letter says:

"We have purchased your debt. You have 30 (thirty) days to dispute the debt or it will be considered valid."

You then have thirty days to respond to the letter. If you do not respond within the specified time frame you lose your right to dispute the debt and by default are obligated to pay the debt.

Let me repeat that:

If you do not respond within the specified time frame you lose your right to dispute the debt and by default are obligated to pay the debt.

Sounds like lawsuit language doesn't it? That's because it is.

Here's what a dunning letter might look like:

> ACME Debt Collection
> 123 Anywhere Lane
> Debtor, IL 12345
>
> Date: June 1, 2010
> Name: John Doe
> Account Number: 1234567
>
> Your account has been reported past due and has been placed with ACME Debt Collection for immediate collection. It is important to contact us as soon as possible. If you are remitting payment, please include your account number on your check or money order. All contacts and payments should be made through this office to ensure proper posting and credit reporting.

For your convenience, you can make a debit or credit card payment by contacting our billing department at 888-DEBTPAY.

Unless you notify this office within 30 days after receiving this notice that you dispute the validity of this debt or any portion thereof, this office will assume the debt is valid. If you notify this office within 30 days from receiving this notice that you dispute this debt or any portion thereof, this office will obtain verification of the debt or obtain a copy of a judgment and mail you a copy of such judgment or verification. If you request this office in writing within 30 days of receiving this notice, this office will provide you with the name and address of the original creditor, if different from the current creditor.

This communication is from a debt collector. This is an attempt to collect a debt, and any information obtained will be used for that purpose.

Sincerely,

Joe Harasser
ACME Debt Collection

Pay special attention to the italicized portion of the sample dunning letter. Once you receive the dunning letter you have 30 days to respond in writing. The FDCPA requires debt collectors, once they have received your dispute letter, *to stop collection efforts and not report anything to the credit bureaus unless or until they verify the debt.*

Quick note: what if you never received a dunning letter and the 30 days has already passed? You may still be okay—just make sure you send a different validation request (a copy of a 30-plus day verification request is provided in the Appendix). This letter states that you never received a dunning letter (or verbal equivalent), and requests verification and validation. This puts you back on the offensive and points out that they are violating the FDCPA by failing to provide a dunning notification in the first place!

Many people stick their heads in the sand when they get a dunning letter and that's exactly what the debt collector hopes you'll do. If you don't respond to a dunning letter within the time limit, your window of opportunity technically closes and you can no longer dispute the debt.

On the other hand, responding causes your rights under the FDCPA to kick in. How should you respond? Just say, in so many words, "I dispute the validity of the debt. Prove it."

If they don't provide the required information, they are prohibited by law to continue collection efforts or report anything to the credit bureaus. It's over (for now). If they do continue, you can sue—or threaten to sue—and use that threat or actual lawsuit as leverage to potentially zero out your account and update your credit report.

Very often debt collectors don't respond to your validation request in an appropriate manner, and instead continue with collection attempts and negative reporting to your credit report (like I said, violating your rights is simply good business.) This is because many debt-buyers simply don't have the information required for proper verification and validation. Often, all they have is your name, account number, and contact information that they bought in bulk from some original creditor or other debt-buyer. We will discuss what constitutes proper validation in later sections along with your options.

After verifying or validating your debt (or immediately if you didn't dispute the debt to begin with), your phone—and possibly your employer's, neighbor's, and family's phones—will start ringing. Official looking letters from what appear to be law firms will start arriving in the mail.

This is where most people start freaking out. Don't.

What you need to realize is that debt collectors are nothing more than sales people (albeit, scary, mean and intimidating ones). They consider you nothing more than a sales lead—you are just a name and a number they want to get money from. Debt collectors buy huge lots of credit card accounts and treat them like ore in a hopper. They need to process a lot of ore to extract the precious metals. To do this they will send out carefully constructed letters (their "marketing materials") that are intended to scare you into paying. Next your phones (and those around you) will blow up trying to hound and guilt you into paying.

However, just like the apple picking analogy above, they are simply shaking the tree and sending in pickers to gather the low-hanging fruit. Whatever remains (the high-hanging fruit) is sold to another debt collector at a huge discount. After all, you have already proven yourself to be difficult and expensive to collect from.

If there is only one idea you take away from this book it should be:

Debt collection is a business like any other, and no business is going to spend its limited time and resources chasing the most difficult clients.

Debt collectors calculate what they can pay for thousands of bad debts and still make money on the deal. They know they will collect on a certain percentage of accounts. They know they won't collect on another percentage. They don't know which *individual* accounts they'll collect on and which they won't. In fact, they don't care—you're just a number, a dollar sign, and a percentage to a debt collector.

Debt collectors try to collect in priority order:

1. Full repayment immediately
2. A payment plan
3. A small "good faith" payment
4. A settlement agreement

It makes sense if you think about it. Best-case scenario the debt collector scares you into paying off the whole account. If that doesn't happen, a full payoff spread out over time isn't bad either; after all, the first few payments probably put the debt collector into the black on your account. Subsequent payments are additional gravy. A settlement agreement is good for the debt collector as well. Having only paid pennies on the dollar for your account, they can take a pretty low-ball offer and still make money from your account. Finally, a "good faith" payment (or any payment for that matter) ensures you have formally acknowledged you owe the debt, and removes some of the rights you'll learn about in the next chapter. Making a good faith payment could also potentially reset the Statute of Limitations on the debt. For these and other reasons, I never recommend making a payment to a debt collector unless you plan on settling the account.

Debt collectors will start with the cheapest tactics, like letters, then move on to more expensive tactics, like phone calls and occasionally lawsuits.

And in the process, they will almost always violate your rights under the FDCPA. Let's find out exactly what your rights are, and how you can start using those rights to your advantage.

Chapter Four
Your Rights Under Federal Law

The debt collection industry is effectively unregulated and definitely out of control. Because most individuals don't know their rights, many debt collectors use illegal tactics to deceive, scare, intimidate, and bully consumers into paying.

Of those few individuals who do understand their rights, even fewer still understand how to correctly document violations and use either the threat of a lawsuit—or an actual suit—to force debt collectors to back off.

Here's the plain truth: violating your rights is simply good business for a debt collector. Even though they might get caught every once in a while, the benefits associated with trampling on your rights far outweigh the penalties they might face. Debt collectors will happily take a few slaps on the wrist if, in the process, they can (and do) make millions.

Well, I am here to put my thumb on the scale by teaching you your rights and how to enforce them—both to hold an unscrupulous industry accountable and to give you additional tools to help get rid of your debt.

The Fair Credit Billing Act

The Fair Credit Billing Act (FCBA) requires creditors to promptly investigate any disputed charges on billing statements and to fix any valid errors without damaging the consumer's credit rating. The FCBA applies to "open ended" credit accounts, like credit cards and revolving charge accounts. The FCBA does not apply to loans with fixed payment schedules, like car loans and home loans.

Among other things, the act creates a process for resolving errors or mistakes. Here's what happens:

1. The consumer must file a written notice of a billing error within sixty days of receiving the bill in question. You must provide enough information to identify yourself and the account, along with the error, the date and amount of the error, and the reasons why you believe the billing is not accurate.

2. The credit card company must then respond to your inquiry within 30 days. The credit card company must resolve the dispute within two billing cycles (typically two months, since most credit card companies bill on a monthly basis), which cannot be longer than 90 days. The credit card company must either explain why the bill is correct, or if it is not correct, fix the error.

3. During the resolution period the credit card company cannot make collection efforts on the *disputed* amount, and cannot charge interest on that amount. They also can't report the account as delinquent to the credit bureaus, and can't close or restrict your account because you have failed to pay the disputed amount.

4. Once the issue is resolved, the credit card company must report the resolution to the credit card bureaus.

If the credit card company does not respond to your inquiry letter, or starts collection proceedings on the amount in question, these are violations of the FCBA and you may have some leverage down the road if you are sued.

Keep in mind that when you dispute a charge the credit card company cannot attempt to collect on the *disputed* amount while the dispute is unresolved: calls, letters, harassment, and threats to report you to the credit bureaus are all violations under the FCBA. Document them! We'll talk more about documentation a little later.

The Fair Debt Collections Practices Act

You may be tempted to skip this section. Please don't.

The Fair Debt Collections Practices Act not only defends your legal rights and protects you from harassment, it can also serve as a playbook for going on the offensive against credit card companies.

Let's get the basics out of the way. The FCBA protects your rights when dealing with original creditors. The FDCPA protects your rights when dealing with debt collectors. Debt collectors are required by the FDCPA to identify themselves as such. If you are being contacted after 180 days of non-payment you can be reasonably sure it is by a debt collector. The FDCPA gives you the right to sue debt collectors who unlawfully threaten, intimidate, berate, or harass you; who call during odd hours; or who falsely represent themselves and their intentions.

See whether debt collectors have done any of the following to you:

- Contacted your employer about a debt you owe

- Called every day, or even several times a day

- Contacted your neighbors about your debt

- Threatened criminal punishment or even arrest

- Threatened you with eviction

- Threatened to sue for costs or fees not allowed by your original agreement or by state law

- Pretended to be a lawyer, government official, or anyone other than who they actually are

FDCPA violations are limited only by the creativity of the debt collectors. Most assume you do not understand your rights, or that, even if you do, you won't act if your rights are violated.

In fact, many debt collectors *themselves* don't know what your rights are and what they are prohibited from doing. If you are contacted by a debt collector about a credit card debt, the person on the other end of the phone is likely to be an under-paid, overworked employee sitting in a massive call center under tremendous pressure to generate revenue. Training is almost nonexistent and job turnover is high.

In short, they don't know your rights and even if they do, they probably don't care.

So what happens if your rights are violated? It depends on the severity of the violation. In addition to fines, you might be entitled to damages. Some collectors have gone so far as to threaten arrest, jail, or harm to loved ones, including informing friends and work associates of the debtor's financial embarrassment. They often threaten wage attachment, even in states that do not allow wages to be garnished. Any threat to take some kind of action that is not allowed by law is an FDCPA violation you can use against the debt collector. We'll talk about how to take action if/when your rights are violated a little later.

FDCPA Basic Rights:

Types of debts covered: Personal, family, and household debts. Unlike the FCBA, this includes open-ended *and* fixed-payment accounts such as personal credit cards, car loans, medical bills, and mortgages. Debts incurred running a business are NOT covered by the FDCPA.

Hours of contact: Debt collectors cannot call before 8 a.m. and after 9 p.m. unless you say so (and why would you?).

Discontinue phone contact: If you want a debt collector to stop calling, simply tell them verbally and follow up in writing. Write a letter, make a copy of the letter, and send it by certified mail, return receipt requested so that you can document that the debt collector received your letter. Once you've notified the debt collector, they can only contact you to let you know they will not contact you again (seems odd, but that's the way it works), or to let you know that they intend to take specific legal action, like filing a suit. Keep in mind "no contact" doesn't mean "no debt"—at this point you still owe the debt. The debt collector just can't call you anymore.

Contacting Others: Debt collectors are only allowed to call or write other people in order to get your *contact information*—they can't state any other purpose for their call. Debt collectors are not permitted to discuss your debt with anyone but you and your spouse (and your attorney if you have one).

Validation rights: If you send the debt collector a request for validation or verification of the debt, they cannot contact you during the interim period, cannot continue collection efforts, and cannot report any negatives to the credit bureaus. Once they do provide validation, they may resume collection and reporting activities.

Income Garnishment: Even if you do lose a lawsuit, many forms of income cannot be garnished. For example, Social Security, pensions, civil service and federal retirement and disability benefits, military pensions and annuities, and even FEMA disaster assistance (check with your state's Attorney General for a complete list) cannot be garnished. If they threaten to go after this income they can't follow through, and threatening means they just violated your rights.

Debt collectors cannot:
- Harass, abuse, or intimidate

- Use obscenities or profanity

- Publish names of people who are in default

- Use the phone to annoy (The FDCPA allows "reasonable" contact frequency. Reasonable is hard to define, but, in general terms, receiving multiple calls a day could be considered annoying and excessive. Some state laws set specific limits.)

Furthermore, debt collectors cannot make false statements including any of the following:

- Claim they work for the government

- Claim they are attorneys (unless they are, of course)

- Claim you've committed a crime

- Claim they work for a credit bureau

- Misrepresent how much money you owe

- Threaten legal action if legal action is not intended (a little hard to prove, admittedly)

- Give inaccurate credit information about you to other parties

- Send documents that look like they come from a government agency or court

- Identify themselves inaccurately (like using a fake company name)

- Say you can be arrested or go to jail for not paying your debts

And you Are NOT required to:

- Answer the phone if a debt collector calls (which is a great use of caller ID)

- Speak with the debt collector if you *do* answer the phone

- Discuss anything with a debt collector that you don't wish to discuss

- Answer any questions about the debt, your finances, your income level, where you live, your monthly expenses, your willingness to pay the debt, or when you'll make your next payment— *in* short *you don't have to answer any questions*

- Be truthful about your financial situation

- And most importantly, *acknowledge that you owe or are in any way responsible for the debt*

If you acknowledge the debt, or make a partial payment, you could extend the time period within which the collector can sue, and you may lose the ability to tilt the playing field back in your favor. **Never acknowledge that you are responsible for the debt, even in the most general or vague terms** (more about that later).

Dunning Letters: Your Rights (and Responsibilities)

We covered dunning letters briefly in the Debt Relief section, but they warrant their own section. Within 5 days of the first communication with you, debt collectors must provide you with a written (or verbal) notice that contains:

1. The amount of the debt

2. The name of the creditor

3. A statement noting the debt will be considered valid unless disputed within 30 days

4. Notice that the debt collector will send a verification and validation of the debt if the request is made within 30 days

Keep in mind there are no formal guidelines for how the dunning letter should be written, other than that the information listed above must be provided in some fashion.

If the debt collector reaches you by phone, the "dunning letter" can be delivered verbally as long as the above items are covered. When that happens, the collector is not required to send a written notice (though most will anyway).

The FDCPA requires that debt collectors verify disputed debts. The reasoning behind this is to make sure the debt collector has matched the right account to the right person. Usually, debt verification and validation will come in the form of photocopies of all of your billing statements. Though the FDCPA is fairly vague on what actually constitutes verification and validation, the verification and validation letter in the Appendix goes one step further. We ask for proof that the debt collector is licensed to collect debts in your state and a copy of any agreement between the original creditor and the debt collector showing their legal right to collect on the alleged debt. After all, anyone can *say* you owe them money. Without providing all of the information requested in our verification and validation letters, there should remain reasonable doubt in your mind as to whether you owe any debt collector anything.

Make sure you send all of your correspondence certified mail with return receipt so that you can prove the debt collector received your debt verification and validation request. Once they receive the request, all collection activities must cease immediately and nothing new can be reported to the credit bureaus until the collections company verifies and validates the debt. There is no time limit for them to respond, but unless and until they do, they must cease all collection activities. If they don't, and/or they continue to report negatives to the credit bureaus, they have just violated your federal rights.

FDCPA violations can help you back down a debt collector by either threatening to sue, or by actually suing them, in federal court. Alternatively, it can serve as an affirmative defense if they try to sue you. You will learn about both of these strategies in later sections. Suffice it to say, it is *very* important that you preserve your rights under the FDCPA by requesting verification and validation of any debt within 30 days of receiving a dunning letter (or verbal equivalent) from a debt collector. Document their response—or lack thereof—and file it away.

That, in a nutshell, is the basics of a dunning letter and your federal rights. So what happens if your rights are violated under the FCBA or FDCPA? It all starts with documentation.

Documenting Violations

If your rights are violated, that can work to your advantage—but only if you *document* those violations. There are several ways to document violations. It is a good idea to use as many as possible, even though that might seem like overkill.

Call logs. Keep a note pad by your phone or visit the Resource Library at DebtClear.com for a call log you can print out. Each time a debt collector calls, write down the following information:

- Person and company calling

- Time and place of call (e.g., work, cell, home, neighbor)

- What was said during the call

- Any potential violations

- How the call made you *feel*—threatened, anxious, can't sleep? This is especially important and may play into potential damages if you end up threatening to sue or actually suing.

Correspondence logs. When you receive correspondence from a debt collector, keep a copy of the correspondence in a file. Keep a separate file for each account. If you send letters or notices in writing, make a copy of those documents and staple them to your certified mail receipt and return receipt proving delivery. Your goal is to have proof of all written correspondence, as well as when anything you sent was received.

Recording calls. If your rights are violated, having actual recordings of those calls is the best evidence. But recorded calls, where all parties are not informed that the call is being recorded, are not admissible in some states.

Here are the basics: Federal law allows the recording of phone calls as long as at least one person (that's you) on the call gives their consent (and you do). Thirty-eight states (and the District of Columbia) agree with federal law. Those states have what is called *one-party consent status*: as long as you are a party to the conversation you may legally record that conversation.

If you live in Nevada, you technically live in a one-party consent state, but the Supreme Court interpreted your state's law to be an all-party law.

The other twelve states require the consent of all parties in a conversation (all-party consent status):

> California
> Connecticut
> Florida
> Illinois
> Maryland
> Massachusetts
> Michigan
> Montana
> Nevada
> New Hampshire

Pennsylvania

Washington

For an up-to-date list of the phone rules in your state, visit http://www.rcfp.org/taping/states.html.

So what does all this mean? If you live in a one-party state, feel free to record your phone conversations without notifying the other party or parties. If you live in an all-party state, the debt collector (and anyone else on the line) must agree to be recorded. If not, those recordings cannot be used as evidence in a court of law. Making recordings is easy. Most electronics stores sell inexpensive phone recording devices, and many newer phones have recording devices already built in!

Keep in mind some people choose to record conversations, even without permission, simply to make note-taking easier. They record the conversation, use that recording to make accurate written notes, and then erase the tape.

Once you document violations it is important to know how serious these violations are. In the Minor FDCPA Violations section below, the violation may be cause for action depending on the nature, severity, and frequency of that violation. Violations from the second section are serious and likely justify an immediate federal complaint. Remember, the more severe the violation, the more leverage you have to force creditors to zero out your account. Keep accurate logs and if you feel your rights have been violated you can get a free consultation from an attorney who specializes in FDCPA violations by visiting DebtClear.com.

Alternatively, you can contact the National Association of Consumer Advocates (www.naca.net) for a referral to an attorney in your state that specializes in creditor issues.

Minor FDCPA Violations

15 U.S.C. 1692g; see 5.7.2.5, supra.	Did the debt collector fail to send a validation notice (aka dunning letter) within five days of the initial communication, whether written or oral?
15 U.S.C. 1692g; see 5.7.3.4, supra.	If the consumer made a timely validation request, did the collector continue collection activities before providing the required validation?
15 U.S.C. 1692e(1); see 5.5.3, supra.	Does the communication give the false impression that the debt collector is affiliated with the United States or any state government, including the use of any badge, uniform, or facsimile of such?
15 U.S.C. 1692e(2); see 5.5.4, supra.	Does the communication contain a false impression of the character, amount, or legal status of the alleged debt?

15 U.S.C. 1692e(5); see 5.5.8, supra.	Does the communication threaten to take any action that cannot legally be taken or that is not intended to be taken (e.g. suit, harm to credit reputation, arrest)?
15 U.S.C. 1692e(7); see 5.5.10, supra.	Does the communication give the false impression that the consumer committed any crime or other conduct in order to disgrace the consumer?
15 U.S.C. 1692e(8); see 5.5.11, supra.	Does the communication communicate or threaten to communicate to any person credit information which is known or which should be known to be false, including the failure to communicate that a disputed debt is disputed?
15 U.S.C. 1692e(9); see 5.5.12, supra.	Does the communication simulate or falsely represent the document to be authorized, issued, or approved by any court, official, or agency of the United States or state government?
15 U.S.C. 1692e preface and e(10); see 5.5.2, 5.5.2.3, supra.	Has the debt collector used any other false, deceptive, or misleading representation or means in connection with the debt collection?

15 U.S.C.1692f(2)-(4); see 5.6.4, supra.	Has the debt collector accepted, solicited, deposited, or threatened to deposit any post-dated check in violation of the Act?
15 U.S.C. 1692f(5); see 5.6.5, supra.	Has the debt collector caused any charges to be made to the consumer, like collect telephone calls?
15 U.S.C. 1692f(7); see 5.6.7, supra.	Has the debt collector communicated by postcard?
15 U.S.C. 1692f(8); see 5.6.8, supra.	Is there any language or symbol other than the debt collector's address on the envelope that indicates that the communication concerns debt collection?
15 U.S.C. 1692d(5); see 5.4.6, supra.	Has the debt collector caused the phone to ring repeatedly or at unreasonable times of the day?
15 U.S.C. 1692d(6); see 5.4.7, supra.	Has the debt collector placed telephone calls without disclosing his/her identity?

15 U.S.C. 1692d preface; see 5.4.1, supra.	Has the debt collector engaged in any other conduct the natural consequence of which is to harass, oppress, or abuse any person in connection with the collection of the alleged debt?
15 U.S.C. 1692c(a)(1); see 5.3.2, supra.	Has the debt collector communicated with the consumer at any unusual time or place known or which should have been known to be inconvenient to the consumer?
15 U.S.C. 1692c(a)(3); see 5.3.4, supra.	Has the debt collector contacted the consumer's place of employment when the debt collector knows or has reason to know that the consumer's employer prohibits such communications?
15 U.S.C. 1692c(c); see 5.3.8, supra.	Has the debt collector contacted the consumer after the consumer has notified the debt collector in writing that the consumer disputes and refuses to pay the debt, or that the consumer wished the debt collector to cease further communication?

Major FDCPA Violations

15 U.S.C. 1692e(4); see 5.5.7, supra.	Does the communication give the impression that nonpayment of any debt will result in the arrest or imprisonment of any person, or the seizure, garnishment, attachment, or sale of any property or wages of any person unless such action is lawful and the debt collector or creditor intends to take such action?
15 U.S.C. 1692b(2); see 5.3.6, supra.	In communications with persons other than the consumer or spouse, has the debt collector stated that the consumer owes any debt?
15 U.S.C. 1692b(3); see 5.3.6, supra.	In communications with persons other than the consumer or spouse, has the debt collector contacted that person more than once?
15 U.S.C. 1692d(1); see 5.4.2, supra.	Has the debt collector used or threatened the use of violence or other criminal means to harm the consumer or his/her property?
15 U.S.C. 1692d(2); see 5.4.3, supra.	Has the debt collector used profane language or other abusive language?

15 U.S.C. 1692d(3); see 5.4.4, supra.	Has the debt collector published a list of consumers who allegedly refuse to pay debts?
15 U.S.C. 1692f preface; see 5.6.1, supra.	Does the collector use any other unfair or unconscionable means to collect or attempt to collect the alleged debt (e.g., collecting time barred debts or filing suit without legal authority)?
15 U.S.C. 1692f(6); see 5.6.6, supra.	Has the debt collector taken or threatened to unlawfully repossess or disable the consumer's property?
15 U.S.C. 1692g; see 5.7.3.4, supra.	Has the collector filed a lawsuit without validating the debt after the consumer has disputed it?

Again, any of the violations above could be cause for legal action. At the very least they can be used to *threaten* legal action and get a debt collector to back down. Even minor violations could result in immediate legal action that may result in fines, penalties, and possibly even elimination of the debt you owe. Some debtors even *make* money by suing abusive debt collectors if the violations are frequent and severe enough! If your rights have been violated, visit DebtClear.com for a free consultation with a FDCPA attorney.

Chapter Five
The FDCPA in Action

Understanding the FDCPA is important. Knowing which violations are more serious than others is also important. Knowing how to deal with debt collectors—and better yet, how to go violation fishing—can be *incredibly* important.

As a reminder, the FDCPA only applies to debt collectors and not original creditors. The original creditor is governed by the Fair Credit Billing Act (FCBA) described earlier. If you're not sure who is calling, a safe rule of thumb to follow is that if it has been more than 6 months since the date of your last payment, you are probably talking to a debt collector.

Let's take a look at a typical debt collector call and how you can use the FDCPA to your advantage.

Aside from getting you to pay the full amount you allegedly owe, a debt collector's immediate goals are to:

1. Get you to admit that the debt is yours

2. Try to get you to make a payment immediately, no matter how small

3. Find out as much information as possible to make their collection efforts easier

Remember, to a debt collector, you're a number. You're a dollar sign. You're not a person.

Regardless of how the debt collector behaves, always be professional and businesslike. If you're harassed, cursed, or treated poorly, don't get mad—just log the particulars so you can prove your rights were violated. Logging and documenting violations is the best way to get even. Remember, you can be sure they are recording the call for "training purposes" even if they don't notify you.

So let's go back to the first phone call you receive. Most debt collectors follow a written script. The debt collection agencies know they have poorly-motivated, poorly-trained employees, so they provide them with written scripts to try to overcome the lack of training and deal with the industry's high turnover rate. Many collectors will quickly veer from the script (if you are going "violation fishing" this is a good thing), but most calls should start the same way.

Sample Debt Collection Call

Debt Collector: "Hello, can I speak to John Doe?"

You: "Can I ask who is calling?" *Always* ask who is calling. FDCPA guidelines specify debt collectors must identify themselves and the company they work for.

Debt Collector: "My name is James Harasser with ACME Collections. We represent Usury Credit Card Company. We are calling to discuss your delinquent VISA account ending in 1234."

You: "Please hold on while I record the call." That is if you choose to record conversations AND you live in an all-party recording state, of course. If you live in a one-party state, you can record away without being obligated to notify the debt collector. In an all-party state, by saying you will turn on your recording device, you give the debt collector the chance to refuse for the call to be recorded.

You: "Thank you. Now that the recording has begun, please state your name, company, phone number, and mailing address as well as the reason for your call?" If you live in a one-party state and are recording the call without the debt collector's knowledge, make sure you ask for this information again once the recording has begun. Whether you are recording the call or not, document the call in your call log.

Debt Collector: (Repeats contact information, etc.)

At this point you can do one of two things:

1. You can state that you don't discuss financial matters on the phone and that if they wish to communicate with you regarding any financial matter they should do so in writing. Then hang up. You should follow up that verbal notice with a formal written request that they stop calling (a sample letter can be found in the Appendix). Send it certified mail with return receipt requested. If they continue to call after they receive the letter, repeat your do-not-call request verbally and record the violation in your call log.

2. Or you can go violation fishing. Remember, now that you know your rights, a violation can be your ally in getting you out of debt. The more documented

violations you have against a collector, the more leverage you have to force them to zero out your debt and cease collection efforts!

So let's say you choose to go violation fishing:

You: "I don't recognize that account, but assuming the account is mine, what are my options? I have never been in this situation before." Remember, you never want to admit the debt is yours, but you also want to give them the chance to violate your rights. *Play dumb*, write down what they say, and compare what they say with the list of FDCPA violations above. When you go violation fishing, you are actually hoping they lie, harass, or even try to intimidate you and call you names—the more the better!

It is also important to note whether you have sent this particular debt collector a notification of dispute and verification/validation request. Remember, a debt collector is required by law to send you a dunning letter within five days of initially contacting you. Often they will send you this letter first, before calling.

Since we recommend you respond to all dunning letters with a dispute and verification/validation request, if the debt collector contacts you without properly answering your dispute, that's another violation. Document it!

Debt Collector: "Oh come on, you know this account is yours. Are you going to take responsibility for what you owe or not?" The debt collector's goal is to push you into acknowledging the debt. If they ask a second time (really, no matter how times they ask), simply restate your position.

You: "Look, I don't have access to my records right now and I have no way of verifying who you are, or whether I might owe you money." Your job is to get the debt collector off script and keep your answers vague and non-committal. Many debt collectors will try to scare, harass, guilt, and intimidate you into paying. Remember, when you go violation fishing you WANT them to violate your FDCPA rights, so play dumb and egg them on. Just make sure you keep in mind to *not admit the debt is yours or give them any additional information such as where you bank, live, or work.*

Debt Collector: "Can I at least get you to verify your address?"

You: "No. There is no way for me to verify who you are so I am not going to give out any personal information over the phone." Why shouldn't you provide your address? If you do, it makes it easier for the debt collector to serve you with a summons if they do decide to take you to court. Giving them banking or employment information makes it that much easier for them to enforce a judgment against you if they get one. Here are some other questions you might hear:

- How much do you bring home every week?

- Is your husband/wife employed? Who does he/she work for? How much does he/she make?

- Do you get child support or alimony?

- Do you own your home or rent?

- How much is your mortgage/rent payment?

- What cars do you own? Do you owe any money on your cars?

- Where do you do your banking?

- Do you have any other loans? How much do you owe?

- Are you behind on your other bills too?

- Can you borrow money from your family or friends?

Of course, it is always within your rights, at any time, to simply tell them you don't want to be contacted by phone anymore and hang up. Just make sure you follow up the verbal request with a written one sent certified mail with return receipt.

You may find yourself in a situation where you catch the debt collector in a violation. Say, for example, that you requested not to be contacted by phone and they continue to call you anyway. Perhaps they have failed to verify and validate the debt and they are still calling and reporting negatives to your credit report. It is perfectly appropriate to tell them—and get it on record—that your rights are being violated. For example:

You: "I disputed the debt you just referred to and have requested verification and validation. Contacting me before satisfying my request violates the FDCPA. If you continue to pursue collection of this debt I will have no choice but to report you to your state Attorney General, the Federal Trade Commission, and to pursue all legal remedies available to me." Then, hang up. Who knows, they might just put you in the high-hanging-fruit category. After all, there are plenty of others out there—who don't understand their rights—who are ripe for the picking!

Watch out for statements like:

Debt Collector: "I know times are tough. Can you at least make a partial payment on this account? Even $10 might help keep my boss off your back for a couple months." Making a partial payment is an acknowledgement you are responsible for the debt and will create a contractual obligation where one didn't exist before (you had a contract with the original creditor, not the debt collector). Furthermore, paying a creditor even a dollar will reset the statue of limitations on your debt.

Debt Collector: "If I can show you a way to pay off this debt without having to go to court, will you be willing to work with me?" Never agree to discuss options unless you are thinking of settling the account. Even then, never admit that the debt is yours (more on this in the section on Debt Settlement).

Bottom line: *never acknowledge or admit to anything, never make a payment to a debt collector unless you intend to settle, and keep good notes in your call log.*

What if Your Rights Have Been Violated?

If your FDCPA rights are violated you can sue in a federal court within one year of the actual date the violation occurred. If you win, the debt collector will be required to pay fines, attorney's fees, court costs, and possibly damages. You can also report the violation to your state Attorney General, their state Attorney General and the Federal Trade Commission (FTC).

Before rushing to make a formal complaint or sue, you should consider *threatening* to complain or sue to force a debt collector to zero out your account and update your credit report accordingly. Why might they be willing to do that? If a debt collector gets enough Attorney General and/or FTC complaints they just might lose their license to operate. Furthermore, the fines, attorney and court fees, and the possibility for damages make going to court very risky, especially if FDCPA violation(s) have clearly occurred. Remember, the debt collector probably paid pennies on the dollar for your account. Writing off your account just makes good business sense when compared with these alternatives.

You can try negotiating a settlement yourself based on FDCPA violations. Alternatively, you can visit DebtClear.com to get a free consultation with an attorney who can evaluate your case and negotiate on your behalf. Depending on your case, an attorney might even take your case on contingency, or just charge a small fee to send a threatening letter to the debt collector demanding they retire your account.

Chapter Six
Your Rights Under State Law

Knowing your rights under Federal law is important, but each state has additional laws that augment your Federal rights. Perform an Internet search for your state's debt collection laws (for example type "Washington State debt collection laws" into your search engine), or visit DebtClear.com for a comprehensive listing of state laws.

Statute of Limitations on Debt Collection

Each state limits how long a debt can be collected. After a set period of time has passed, an unpaid debt is considered by law to be a "time-barred debt" and is uncollectable. More precisely, the debt collector can still try to collect the debt, but they cannot sue you for it. Without the ability to sue, the most a creditor can do is report the delinquent account on your credit report for up to seven years. The clock starts ticking from the day you last made a payment on that account and the clock gets reset if you make a payment, even a partial payment! This is why I do not recommend making any payments on delinquent accounts unless you are prepared to settle the account.

To determine what the statute of limitation is in your state, consult the chart below and confirm with your state's Attorney General's office.

Alabama	3 years
Alaska	3 years

Arizona	3 years
Arkansas	5 years (2 years for medical debt)
California	4 years
Colorado	6 years
Connecticut	6 years
Delaware	3 years
District of Columbia	3 years
Florida	5 years
Georgia	4 years
Hawaii	6 years
Idaho	5 years
Illinois	10 years
Indiana	6 years
Iowa	5 years
Kansas	5 years
Kentucky	5 years
Louisiana	3 years
Maine	6 years
Maryland	3 years
Massachusetts	6 years
Michigan	6 years
Minnesota	6 years
Mississippi	3 years
Missouri	5 years
Montana	8 years
Nebraska	4 years
Nevada	4 years
New Hampshire	3 years
New Jersey	6 years

New Mexico	4 years
New York	6 years
North Carolina	3 years
North Dakota	6 years
Ohio	6 years
Oklahoma	3 years
Oregon	6 years
Pennsylvania	4 years
Rhode Island	10 years
South Carolina	3 years
South Dakota	6 years
Tennessee	6 years
Texas	4 years
Utah	4 years
Virginia	3 years
Vermont	3 years
Washington	6 years
West Virginia	5 years
Wisconsin	6 years
Wyoming	8 years

Make sure you consult your actual state statute and verify the times listed above (search the internet for "unsecured debt statute of limitations yourstate"). Some states start the clock from the date of your first missed payment, while others start the clock from the date the original creditor charges-off your account (usually six months after the date of your first missed payment).

If a debt collector contacts you after your state's statute of limitations has expired, write a letter (certified mail with return receipt) to the debt collector stating that the account is no longer collectible and instruct them to cease all communication and collection efforts (a sample letter can be found in the Appendix or Resource Library at DebtClear.com). If you are sued by a creditor after your state's statute of limitations has expired, simply provide the court a copy of your state's statute and a copy of your credit report showing the date of your first missed payment and/or the date of charge-off by the original creditor.

Keep in mind that after the statute of limitations has expired on your debt, it can still be legally reported on your credit report for up to seven years. However, a time-barred debt is less likely to be verified by the creditor and is therefore easier to remove through a formal dispute with the credit bureaus.

If you live in a state with a long statute of limitations period, don't despair. In my experience if you are going to be sued, it will most likely happen in the first couple of years. The reason is because your collection account diminishes in value to a debt collector over time. Since the most expensive collection activity is to sue, chances are a debt collector will sue—if they are going to—while the account is still fresh. That is not to say that you won't be sued after a couple of years, but the odds drop off dramatically over time.

Now that you know the major players, how debt collection works, and more importantly your state and federal rights, it's time to put it all together.

Chapter Seven
Putting It All Together

I realize many of you might have skipped directly to this section first. Maybe you saw our guarantee and thought, "How can this program be so effective?"

If this is you, then please go back and read the previous six chapters. You absolutely must understand the various components of the program before I can tell you how to put them all together.

Once you've read chapters 1 – 6 you're ready to get down to brass tacks.

Debt Relief Overview

Here is our debt relief process in a nutshell:

1. Stop (for whatever reason) making payments to your creditors.

2. Protect your assets.

3. Start repairing your credit.

4. Start saving all the money you can.

5. Respond to all dunning letters with a dispute and verification/validation request.

6. Document all communications along with any FDCPA violations.

7. Sue or threaten to sue a debt collector if your rights are violated.

8. Respond to lawsuits with the required information and within the timeframe specified.

9. Settle if you can't shake a lawsuit.

10. Continue to repair your credit.

Topics like dealing with lawsuits, protecting assets, and repairing credit are covered in separate sections of this book, but I've included them here to round out the process so you can see it from start to finish.

For a more detailed look at the process, check out the Roadmap section of this book or on the DebtClear.com website.

It is important to note that there are only two ways for a creditor to collect money from you:

1. Sue you, *and* win, *and* find any assets, income, or bank accounts, *and* enforce the judgment. OR

2. You voluntarily pay them.

Number one above costs debt collectors a lot of money with no guarantee they will get a return on their investment. As a rule, those who default on their unsecured debt don't have much to collect on in the first place. With over 80% of judgments going uncollected[10], you can see why most debt collectors don't bother

---

[10] The Kaulkin Report; 5th Edition

suing—the margins are very slim. Instead, most debt collectors use scare tactics, guilt, intimidation, shame, and coercion to collect the majority of their money. Those tactics are cheap, and work on a large percentage of the population.

That's why they go after low-hanging fruit.

Your goal is to become high-hanging fruit. My goal is to help you. Every technique and strategy outlined in this book is designed to move you higher up in the tree!

What debt collectors don't want you to know is that *there is actually very little they can do to you when it comes to unsecured debts*. They know it. And now you know it.

Now, this is *not* to say that if a debt collector receives a judgment against you they cannot garnish your wages, put liens on your property, or take money from your bank accounts because they can do all of these things. They can also charge post-judgment interest and may even be able to renew any judgments.

That's why we will also teach you how to protect your assets and fight creditor lawsuits.

Finally, by understanding your rights under the FDCPA when (notice I didn't say "if") they do harass and intimidate you and otherwise violate your rights, you can identify and legally document these violations and use them as leverage to potentially zero out your accounts and update your credit report. If you don't understand your rights go back and read that section. Knowledge is power and knowing your rights is the first step towards gaining that power.

Now, back to the process:

1. **First, you stop (for whatever reason) making payments and save as much money as you can.** Within a short period of time …

2. **Original creditors will start calling.** You can answer the phone if you like, or just let it go to voicemail.

3. **At some point the original creditor is likely to offer a settlement.** It is up to you to decide whether to take it or leave it. If you want to try settling the account on your own, check out the tutorial in the Roadmap section of this book. You may also consider enlisting the help of a professional. You can find a trusted and accredited negotiation professional at DebtClear.com.

4. **Occasionally an original creditor will sue.** If that happens, you may consider using some of the money you've saved to settle the account. After reading the section on Asset Protection you may find that you are actually collection proof and a judgment is of little consequence to you.

5. **Original creditors will usually write off the debt after six months and debt collectors will take over.** Answer the phone, assert your rights under the FDCPA, document all calls, listen closely for violations and never, ever acknowledge the debt, make a payment (unless settling the account), or give out any personal information. If you prefer, send

a certified letter telling them not to call you. I recommend you go violation fishing, but the choice is obviously yours.

6. **Settle if you choose to, don't if you don't.** The benefit of settling the account is that collection efforts stop and you can usually have your credit report updated to "paid as agreed," or have the tradeline removed altogether as part of the settlement agreement. The choice is always yours, but I don't recommend settling unless you have to. For obvious reasons, this will also void the limited money-back guarantee that comes with this book.

7. **Wait for the statute of limitations to expire** and you're debt free!

8. **Finally, continue to repair any damage to your credit.** The process of credit repair really should start once the original creditor writes off the debt. The older the debt, the less likely it is to be reinserted if you have the negative tradeline successfully removed. However, there isn't any downside to starting sooner than later.

When Will Your Debts Be Eliminated?

A question I'm frequently asked is, "When will my debts be eliminated?" The answer is a bit involved.

I would first like to answer the question with another question: "If a debt collector cannot collect on an account, and that account no longer appears on your credit report, has it been eliminated?" The answer effectively is, "Yes!" Though the account may exist somewhere out there in the ether, it has no real relevance to your life.

The second part of the answer has to do with your state's statute of limitations on collecting unsecured debt. If you can remain judgment free until the statute of limitations has expired on your debt, then the debt is uncollectable, and, again, has effectively been eliminated.

The third part of the answer is that if you have documented violations of the FDCPA by a debt collector, you can go on the offensive and force them to zero out your accounts and update your credit report as already described. Result: debt eliminated.

The fourth part of the answer depends on if you settle the account. To maximize debt relief, I don't recommend settling unless you are sued and can't have the case dismissed. However, some of you might choose this route if you have the money for the "sleep-at-night" factor it affords. Either way, the debt (or a portion thereof) is effectively eliminated.

Next Steps

The steps outlined above are intended to be an overview of the debt relief process. However, the real nuts and bolts section of this book is the Roadmap section. This section assumes that you have read all the other sections of this book (Credit Repair, Debt Relief, Lawsuits, and Asset Protection) before putting it all together.

In the meantime, you can start putting what you learned in this section to good use, especially when dealing with debt collectors and enforcing and maintaining your FDCPA rights.

Credit Repair

Chapter Eight
Do-It-Yourself Credit Repair

The credit repair industry is a multi-million dollar business.

Why? Your credit score is used to determine a variety of factors including whether you are hired for a job, whether you qualify for insurance or a home loan, and, most importantly, the rate at which you can borrow money. For major purchases like a car or home, having a better credit score can literally translate to a difference of thousands of dollars in interest payments alone.

Of course, there are legitimate and reputable credit repair companies you can turn to (visit DebtClear.com for recommendations). But what most other credit repair companies won't tell you is *they can't do anything for you that you can't do yourself*!

The average credit repair company simply sends out generic form letters. In essence, they throw a lot of paper at the credit bureaus' walls and hope a few stick. These credit repair companies seldom look for specific problems *within* items to dispute, look for discrepancies between credit reports from different bureaus, or send supporting documentation. They just plug and chug.

Furthermore, no credit repair company I know of sends disputes to the credit bureaus by certified mail with return receipt. Without proof of delivery, there is no recourse if a bureau fails to respond to a dispute in a timely manner. Sadly, millions of negative records remain on credit reports that could have otherwise been removed if proof of delivery could have been demonstrated.

This section will teach you all of the insider tricks that credit repair companies use, and even some they don't! By the time you are finished reading this section you will know more than most "professional" credit repair companies out there. However, if you want to have a reputable company repair your credit for you, just visit DebtClear.com for a referral.

Why You Can, and Should, Do-It-Yourself

1. The overwhelming majority of credit repair companies simply dispute negative entries on your credit report in the hopes that the credit reporting agencies won't be able to verify the information with creditors and will be forced to remove those entries from your credit report. Although 70 – 90% of all credit reports include some errors, the vast majority of negative entries on the average credit report are in fact valid. Since most credit repair companies simply dispute negative entries on your report, those entries will most likely be verified by the credit reporting agencies and will not be deleted.

2. Using a credit repair company that simply disputes tradelines is like playing the slots: your hope is that all three bureaus will be unable to verify the entries in a timely or appropriate manner. More than likely, if a valid negative entry is removed at all, it will only be removed from a single bureau's report and can easily be reinserted.

3. Most credit repair companies don't teach you how to BUILD your credit.

4. By law, no one but you is allowed to dispute any information on your credit file. Many credit repair companies have to "pretend" to be you when they send dispute requests to the credit bureaus. If the credit bureau determines that someone other than you is disputing information on your credit report, they are entitled to deny the request.

5. Best of all, you can do all of this yourself for the price of postage and proof of delivery!

All you need now are a few simple rules from the Fair Credit Reporting Act, an understanding of how your credit score is calculated, and the insider credit repair techniques outlined in this book.

Why You Must Take Action: The Consequences of Bad Credit

A poor credit history and a low credit score can have a devastating effect on your finances and on your lifestyle. I cannot stress enough the importance of erasing bad credit, increasing your credit score, and regularly monitoring your credit report for fraudulent activity. Your credit score creates a virtual reputation that can have far-reaching and sometimes unexpected consequences. Let's look at a few.

Increased Fees & Penalties

Falling behind on credit payments can result in late fees, over-limit fees, legal fees, repossession fees, penalty fees, deficiency payments, and default rates. In fact, creditors often charge fees even before they extend you credit based upon your credit score:

you might be charged a set-up fee, a monthly maintenance fee, an annual fee, or a new customer fee.

Higher Interest Rates

The lower your credit score, the higher your interest rate—and the difference can be significant. At first glance, the differences in monthly payments in the chart below may not look significant. However, if you have a credit score between 620 and 639 you'll pay more than $110,000 in additional interest over the life of the loan than a person with a credit score above 760!

Sample of the Interest Rate on a 30-Year Fixed Mortgage for
$300,000

FICO® score	APR	Monthly payment
760-850	5.404%	$1,685
700-759	5.626%	$1,727
680-699	5.803%	$1,761
660-679	6.017%	$1,802
640-659	6.447%	$1,886
620-639	6.993%	$1,994

Even something minor like having too many account inquiries in your file, or carrying a high balance on your credit card, can drop your score.

Loss of Employment Opportunities

Many potential employers review your credit report to determine your suitability for hire. Why? Many people feel the way a person manages their finances is a reflection of how they handle other areas of their life, including work. They view potential employees with a bad credit history as potentially unreliable and unproductive. Conversely they view prospective employees with good credit as responsible, productive, and trustworthy.

Increased Insurance Premiums

The guys at the insurance companies who crunch numbers and look for trends will tell you there is a strong correlation between clients with bad credit and the number of reported insurance claims. The result of their findings: if you have bad credit, you'll be charged a higher premium and may even be denied insurance altogether.

Inability to Rent Property

If you have your eye on renting a new apartment, your credit history may affect the acceptance of your application. Almost without exception, landlords perform a credit check. They look for late payments, missed payments, or defaults on your credit report. To a landlord, your payment history is a good indication of how you will pay, regardless of whether you have a stable income or outstanding references.

Inability to Buy a Home

The number one indicator of financial stability and net worth is whether or not an individual owns a home. A bad credit score can keep this aspect of the American Dream permanently out of your reach.

Chapter Nine
What Is Credit?

Credit begins with you, the *debtor*. If you wish to purchase something now and pay for it later, one way is to apply for credit with a *creditor* (or lender). Your payment history is then reported to the credit bureaus by your creditors and becomes part of your credit report and score. There are many types of credit available, but most fall into two basic categories:

1. Secured Credit: secured credit involves, you guessed it, *security*. The credit is secured with real property—like a house, a vehicle, or some other tangible asset—and the lender is protected if you should default on your loan. Under default, they can repossess the property tied to the loan. Secured credit usually comes with lower interest rates and longer terms because it's less risky for a lender.

2. Unsecured Credit: unsecured credit is backed only by your promise to repay the debt. The lender faces greater risk and for that reason unsecured credit usually comes with higher interest rates and shorter terms. Most credit card accounts, signature loans, and lines of credit fall into this category.

In order to determine whether you are a good credit risk, the lender conducts a credit check by contacting one of the three major credit bureaus: Equifax, Experian, or TransUnion. Besides the "Big Three" credit bureaus, there are many other specialty credit bureaus, but for the most part creditors obtain consumer credit information from one or more of the three major bureaus. The credit bureaus provide lenders with a credit report that contains information on your credit and payment history along with a credit score. A credit score is a numerical rating based on the information on your credit report, and is used to quickly tell the lender how likely you are to default on a loan.

As you can now see, your credit report and credit score makes all the difference in whether or not you will be approved for a loan, and under what terms. Since 70 – 90% of all credit reports include some number of errors, the government has created legislation allowing you to dispute incorrect, outdated, and/or incomplete information. In addition, agencies were created to regulate and oversee the industry as a whole—both the reporters of credit information and the credit bureaus themselves. Guidelines for regulating the industry and protecting your rights are spelled out in the Fair Credit Reporting Act.

What Is the Fair Credit Reporting Act?

The Fair Credit Reporting Act (FCRA) is a set of federal laws that regulates how a consumer's credit information is collected, shared, and used. The FCRA promotes accuracy, fairness, and privacy by outlining the responsibilities of:

- Consumer Reporting Agencies (CRAs): credit bureaus, like Experian, TransUnion, and Equifax that report your credit information to creditors, employers, landlords, insurance companies, etc.

- Furnishers of credit information: usually your creditors, but also collection agencies, employers, and courts, all of which can provide your credit information to the consumer reporting agencies.

- Users of credit information: businesses and individuals that extend credit, insurance, employment, apartments for rent, etc.

Your Rights: How the FCRA Helps You

So why should you care about the FCRA? Understanding and using the provisions of the FCRA is the basis of the credit repair process. With a clear understanding of the rules contained within the FCRA and how to use those rules to your advantage, you can remove almost any negative entry from your credit report. Though the intent of the FCRA is to allow you to remove outdated or inaccurate information, it can also be used to remove negative items that are valid but that contain reporting errors. There are over 40 pieces of information that each of your entries should contain. If any piece of information is missing or inaccurate and is not updated in a timely or appropriate manner, then the *entire entry must be removed!* (Coincidentally, the Federal Trade Commission doesn't allow credit repair companies to state that valid negative entries can be removed using the FCRA. Good thing I'm not a credit repair company!)

Here is a brief description of your rights under the FCRA:

- **You have the right to review your credit file.** Upon request, the credit reporting agencies are required to provide you with a copy of your credit report. You may receive one free credit report per year. Additional copies are available for a fee.

- **You have the right to receive your credit score.** A credit score is a number used to rate your credit worthiness. For a nominal fee, you may obtain your current credit score from the credit reporting agencies.

- **You must be notified if information in your credit report is used to deny you credit, insurance, or employment.** If you are denied, you may also, at no charge, request a copy of the credit report that served as the basis for denying you credit.

- **You have the right to dispute inaccurate or outdated information in your credit report**, and the consumer reporting agencies are required to investigate those disputes.

- **Consumer reporting agencies must correct or delete inaccurate, incomplete, or un-verifiable information within 30 days.**

- **Consumer reporting agencies cannot report negative information about you that is outdated**—this means information that is more than seven years old, or a bankruptcy or tax lien that is more than ten years old.

- **Access to your credit file is restricted** only to those who have a verifiable need, such as creditors, employers, and insurers.

- **Employers, or potential employers, are not allowed to review your credit report without your written approval.**

- **You have the right to sue** anyone who violates the FCRA.

But wait, there's more!

The FACT Act

The Fair and Accurate Credit Transactions (FACT) Act of 2003 provides additional consumer protection. It redefines and sets new credit-reporting standards for accuracy, privacy, limits on information sharing, and consumer rights to disclosure. The FACT Act expands your rights, protects your identity, and grants you more power regarding your credit report. Here's what the FACT Act does:

- **Allows you to receive free copies of your credit report** if you have suffered an adverse action based on your credit file.

- **Requires your consent** before anyone may view your credit report or specialty reports that contain your personal medical information.

- **Requires creditors to inform you** if they place any negative information in your file.

- **Lets you place a 100-word statement** in your file to explain any extenuating circumstances or details about specific disputes or negative entries.

- **If your identity is stolen,** allows you to place a fraud alert and freeze your credit file by simply calling one of the credit bureaus.

- **Allows you to sue and receive damages** from anyone who violates the FACT Act.

Each state also maintains its own laws related to credit reporting. Visit your state Attorney General's website for additional state-by-state information.

Chapter Ten
What is a Credit Score?

Back in the 1950s, a company called Fair Isaac Corporation created a modeling method to predict consumer payment behavior. As a result, the credit score was born. A credit score is a three-digit number ranging from 300 to 850 that summarizes your risk of default. A credit score is a key component used in most credit reviews performed today.

There are two main types of credit scores: FICO and VantageScore. In addition, there are a number of proprietary credit scoring models, like NextGen, BEACON, and EMPIRICA. In almost every case your credit-worthiness will be evaluated using a credit score calculated by FICO or VantageScore.

What Affects Your Credit Score?

Your credit rating is affected by your payment history, the total amount you owe all creditors, your debt to available credit ratio, the types of credit you have, how long you've had credit, and how much new credit you've received or recently applied for.

Let's look a little closer at each component of your credit rating:

- **Payment History** takes into account how you have paid your creditors over the past 7 years—if you pay on time as agreed, made late payments, or defaulted on a loan.

- **Balances** considers how much you owe your creditors and how many high balances you carry.

- **Ratio of Debt to Credit** is the percentage you owe on an account compared to the account's total credit limit. When you owe more than 50% of the credit limit your credit score is adversely affected. As a general rule, your goal should be to keep your balance below 50% of the total credit limit. Below 30% of the credit limit is even better. (Though not a part of your credit score, most lenders will also look at your overall debt to income ratio—short, how much you owe versus how much you earn. The lower the ratio the better.)

- **Types and Diversity of Credit** means the kind of credit you carry, such as revolving credit (the riskiest type of credit), or secured credit (the safest type of credit). According to the credit bureaus an ideal number of entries is made up of two installment accounts (like a mortgage and an auto loan) and two revolving accounts (like credit cards, store cards, gas cards, etc.).

- **Credit History**. The longer you have had positive credit accounts, which remain open and active, the higher your credit score.

- **New Credit and Inquiries**. Every time you apply for new credit, or ask for an increase in credit, your credit score is adversely affected. Credit and collection agency inquiries are considered "hard pulls" and lower your credit score. According to credit industry statistics, six or more recent inquiries on your credit report implies you will be eight times more likely to file for bankruptcy than if you had no inquiries in your file. Receiving promotional offers or requesting your own report or score are considered "soft pulls" and do not affect your score.

Even though "soft pulls" do not affect your credit score, if you wish to opt out of pre-screened offers you can do so by submitting your contact information at www.optoutprescreen.com.

What Does *Not* Affect Your Credit Score:

- Age, Gender, or Income

- Inquiries made by you to review your own credit score or credit report

- Inquiries made for the same type of credit, such as for a mortgage or car loan within a 14-day period—this allows you to comparison shop for financing without your credit score taking a big hit (keep in mind this grace period does not extend to credit card inquiries)

- Your spouse's credit score or credit history—any joint credit accounts you hold with your spouse will appear on both of your credit reports and affect both of your credit scores, but your and your spouse's credit scores are not merged

Credit Scoring Models

So how is your credit score determined? FICO and VantageScore use slightly different scoring models.

The FICO score is the most widely used by creditors. The FICO score ranges from 300 to 850. The higher your score, the better your credit rating. Your FICO score is made up of five components:

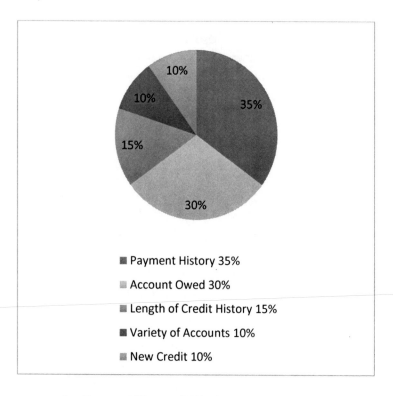

1. **Payment History** (35% of score)

   This section includes payments made on time as well as the number of late payments (including how many late payments you have and the dollar amount of the late payments). Recent activity has a larger impact on your score than older activity.

2. **Amounts Owed** (30% of score)

   This section includes the total amount you owe, the amount you owe by account type (such as revolving, installment, or mortgage), the number of accounts on which you're carrying a balance, and the proportion of the available credit lines used. To receive a high number in this category, you should have a low balance owed in relation to the amount of credit available. For installment credit, your proportion of balance is defined as the amount remaining on the loan in relation to the original amount of the loan. For revolving credit, your proportion of balance is defined as the amount you currently owe in relation to your credit limit.

3. **Length of Credit History** (15% of score)

   A longer credit history increases your credit score. This is both the age of your active accounts and the length of your credit history across all accounts.

4. **Variety of Accounts** (10% of score)

   In an ideal situation you will use a mix of different types of credit. If you carry a high-percentage of risky types of credit, such as revolving credit (credit cards) or finance-company loans, your score will be lower than if you debt is from more secure credit, such as car loans or mortgage loans.

5. **New Credit** (10% of score)

   This category takes into account the types and number of new (and increased) credit lines, which includes applications for credit. The more new, requested, or increased credit you have, the lower your score in this category. Why? Fair Isaac assumes that if you apply for more credit (and especially for several new accounts at the same time) you may be living beyond your means and will be unable to afford to pay off the debt.

On March 14, 2006, the "big-three" credit bureaus created another model, VantageScore, for use as a common scoring product method, although they each still offer their own proprietary scoring methods as well. The VantageScore numerical range is 501 to 990.

Your VantageScore is determined by six components:

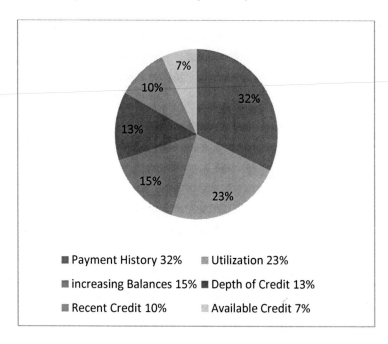

■ Payment History 32% ▒ Utilization 23%
▒ increasing Balances 15% ■ Depth of Credit 13%
■ Recent Credit 10% ▒ Available Credit 7%

1. **Payment History** (32% of score)

   As with the FICO score, your payment history is the most significant element in determining your VantageScore credit score.

2. **Utilization** (23% of score)

   This is the percentage of your available credit that you have used. Using a smaller proportion of your available credit has a positive affect on your credit rating.

3. **Increasing Balances** (15% of score)

   Recent increases in your balances indicates greater risk and lowers your score.

4. **Depth of Credit** (13% of score)

   This means how long you've had credit, along with the types of credit you hold.

5. **Recent Credit** (10% of score)

   This is the number of credit accounts you have recently opened and new inquiries you have made. Initially, when new credit appears on your record it will lower your score. Over time, if you keep new accounts in good standing, they can actually help increase your credit score, especially if you keep your utilization rate low.

6. **Available Credit** (7% of score)

   This is the amount of credit available on *all* your accounts. The more credit available (and the less used) the higher your credit score.

What Is a Good Credit Score?

What is considered a "good score" changes over time, depending on changes in the overall population's credit and payment history. No matter what the current "good range," think of a "good credit score" as a score that allows you to obtain credit at an affordable rate.

Below is a current bar chart showing the national distribution of FICO scores. Take a look and see where you stand.

National Distribution of FICO Scores

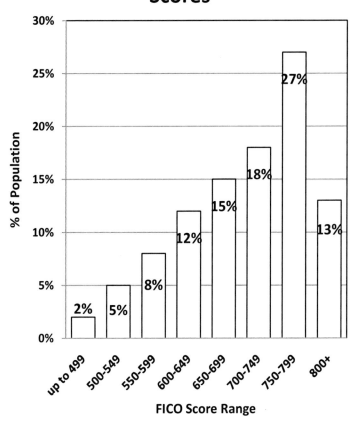

VantageScore uses a grading system scale to estimate your ranking:

Grade	Name	Score Range	Percentage of Population
A	Super Prime	901 to 990	15%
B	Prime	801 to 900	50%
C	Near Prime	701 to 800	25%
D	Sub-Prime	501 to 700	10%

Obtaining Your Credit Score

Remember, because there are different credit bureaus, you will always have more than one credit score. You will have at least four credit scores: your FICO Score, your VantageScore, and the credit bureaus' proprietary scores. Equifax uses BEACON, TransUnion uses EMPIRICA, and Experian uses VantageScore. Each of your credit scores will be different because each of the credit bureaus maintains separate files of your credit history, and not all creditors report to each bureau.

The credit bureaus charge an additional fee (not to exceed $9.00) to provide your credit score along with your credit report.

Chapter Eleven
What Is a Credit Report?

A credit report details a consumer's borrowing and repayment history. Each of the three big credit bureaus—Equifax, Experian, and TransUnion—provide credit reports to your creditors and others, such as potential employers, landlords, and insurance companies, who seek information about your credit history.

Who Is Allowed to Get a Copy of Your Credit Report?

If a business or individual has a valid reason to review your report *and* has your permission to do so, they can get a copy of your report. Keep in mind you might not know you're giving permission; your "permission" is often included in the fine print of the credit card, loan, or employment application you sign.

Here's a quick summary of who can review your report:

- **Creditors**: Anyone you ask to grant you credit, including for a credit card, a car loan, a student loan, or a mortgage

- **Landlords**: If you submit an application to rent an apartment

- **Employers**: If you submit a job application

- **Insurance Companies**: If you apply for insurance, including auto, homeowner's, renter's, and medical insurance

- **Professional Licensers**: If you apply for certain professional licenses, including investment banking, stock trading, and gambling licenses

- **The Courts**: Your credit record can be viewed by court order or subpoena

- **Collection Agencies**: If you have defaulted on an account and it is sold to a third-party debt collector

- **Internal Revenue Service**: If you owe the IRS money

- **You**: Last, but definitely not least, you are allowed to review your own file (see the section below on Obtaining Your Credit Report)

How Negative Information Gets on Your Credit Report

All the information on your credit report is supplied to the credit bureaus by your lenders, employers, bill collectors, courts, public utilities, and anyone else who supplies you credit.

The Fair and Accurate Credit Transactions Act (FACT Act) requires that you be notified if negative information about you is reported to a credit bureau. Your creditor (or third-party debt collector) must send you a one-time notice either before, or no later than 30 days after, negative information (late payments, missed payments, partial payments, or other defaults) is given to a credit bureau. This notification rarely happens and can be a factor in your favor in some of our debt relief and lawsuit strategies.

How Long Does Information Stay on Your Credit Report?

Most entries made in credit reports have a limited lifespan and must be removed from the credit file after that time has elapsed.

TYPE OF ACCOUNT	TIME LIMIT ON CREDIT REPORT
Credit Accounts in good standing	Up to 10 years
Credit Accounts in bad standing	7 years
Collection Activity	7 years
Charge-Offs	7 years
Unpaid Judgments	7 years from filing date or until the statute of limitations expires (whichever is longer)
Paid Tax Liens	7 years
Unpaid Tax Liens	No time limit

IRS Liens	Until removed by the IRS
Bankruptcies (Chapter 7, 10, 11, & 13)	7-10 years
Employer Inquiries (for salaries greater than $75,000)	No time limit
Insurance Inquiries (for policies greater than $150,000)	No time limit

What Is Included in Your Credit Report?

You will find the following information in each of your credit reports:

1. **Personal Identification Information**
   - Name
   - Social security number
   - Birth date
   - Past and present addresses
   - Recent employment history

2. **Public Record Information**
   - Tax liens
   - Bankruptcies
   - Foreclosures
   - Judgments
   - Child support orders

3. **Individual Credit Account Information**
   - Whether they are open or closed
   - The name of the lender you owe
   - What type of account it is
   - Whether it is a joint account (shared with another person, such as a spouse) or individually held
   - The outstanding balance
   - The amount of your monthly payment
   - Whether you've paid late or on time
   - Your credit limit

4. **List of Inquiries**

   The names of companies or individuals who requested your credit report for the purpose of granting you credit.

5. **100 Word Statement (optional)**

   An optional message you can write and submit, used to explain any extenuating circumstances related to negative information in your credit report.

6. **Credit Score (optional)**

   An add-on you may request.

How Do You Read Your Credit Report?

Each credit report differs in its appearance, but contains the same basic information, usually divided into four sections:

1. **Identifying Information**

2. **Account History**

   May be sub-divided into two sections: positive accounts and collection accounts.

3. **Public Records**

4. **Inquiries**

   Divided into two categories: hard and soft inquiries.

Your personal profile details, public records section, and list of credit inquiries are self-explanatory and easy to read. The account history section is a little trickier to follow if you've never seen a credit report. Following is a breakdown showing how each of the three main credit bureaus lists the account history section.

Experian Credit Report

Experian groups accounts into categories like "Accounts in Good Standing" and "Potentially Negative Items." Each account is listed alphabetically by creditor. For security purposes, the full account number is not provided in the report, so other people don't have access to your account numbers. Here's what appears in the Experian Account History section:

- **Status**—open or closed account
- **Date Open**—the date the account was opened
- **Reported Since**—first reported date
- **Date of Status**—when the status was updated
- **Last Reported**—when the last update was reported
- **Account Type**—installment, revolving, or mortgage
- **Terms**—the number of payments in your payment plan
- **Monthly Payment**—the latest reported minimum payment due
- **Responsibility**—who has to make the payments (individual or joint)
- **Credit Limit**—the highest amount you have been approved to use
- **High Balance**—the highest amount you've ever owed on the account
- **Recent Balance Information**—the current total amount you owe
- **Recent Payment**—the most recent payment you made on the account
- **Account History**—indicates whether you have paid on time or late
- **Your Statement**—optional section where you can write a response to the account history information
- **Account History**—this section repeats as an optional response by the creditor to any statement you may have placed on the credit report

Equifax Credit Report

Equifax reports its "Account History" by type of account, such as mortgages, revolving credit, installment accounts, etc. Equifax shortens account numbers to protect your privacy. Equifax provides a short summary before each account listing, including your "Account Status," which indicates whether you have paid the account as agreed or defaulted. An Equifax account history looks like this:

- **Account Number**—the number used to identify the credit card or loan
- **Account Owner**—who is responsible for the account (individual or joint)
- **Type of Account**—installment, revolving, other, or collections
- **Term Duration**—the total number of payments in your repayment plan
- **Date Open**—the date the account was opened
- **Date Reported**—when the lender last reported on the account
- **Date of Last Payment**—the last time you made a payment on the account
- **Scheduled Payment Amount**—lists the amount due each month on an installment account
- **Creditor Classification**—indicates the type of creditor
- **Charge-Off Amount**—the amount of any debt that was not paid by you that the lender wrote off as uncollectible

- **Balloon-Payment Amount**—the amount of the lump-sum payment at the end of the loan term (some loans will not have this payment)
- **Date Closed**—when you closed the account
- **Date of First Delinquency**—when you first defaulted on your payment plan
- **Comments**—additional information about the account supplied by the creditor
- **Current Status**—indicates if you are paying on time or are past due
- **High Credit**—indicates the highest amount of credit you have ever used on the account
- **Credit Limit**—the highest amount of credit available for the account
- **Term's Frequency**—indicates when your payment is due (monthly, weekly, quarterly, etc.)
- **Balance**—the total current amount owed on the loan
- **Amount Past Due**—the amount that was due but has not been paid
- **Actual Payment Amount**—the amount of money you paid on the due amount
- **Date of Last Activity**—when you last used the account
- **Months Reviewed**—how many months are reviewed and included on the credit report (Equifax maintains up to 81 months of an account's history)
- **Activity Description**—indicates if it is paid, closed, etc.

- **Deferred Payment Start Date**—indicates the start date to begin paying on a deferred loan (such as a promotional loan or student loan)
- **Balloon-Payment Date**—when the lump-sum amount is due at the end of your loan term
- **Type of Loan**—indicates if it's a credit card, auto loan, etc.
- **81-Month Payment History**—outlines each month's payment status for up to seven years of account history (notations include "pays as agreed," VS for voluntary surrender, F for foreclosure, R for repossession, CO for charge-off, CA for collection account; a number, such as 30 or 60, indicates a range of days past due

TransUnion Credit Report

On the TransUnion report, your "Account History" is grouped into "Adverse Accounts" and "Satisfactory Accounts." TransUnion displays the account numbers in full. Contact information for the creditor (mailing address and telephone number) is typically included. A Transunion "Account History" section looks like this:

- **Loan Type**—indicates if the debt is a credit card, mortgage, auto loan, line of credit, etc.
- **Late Payments**—grouped under 30, 60, or 90 days old
- **Remark**—indicates if the account is open or closed
- **Balance**—the current total balance on the account
- **Date Updated**—when the lender last reported information on the account

122

- **High Balance**—the highest amount you have ever owed on the account
- **Collateral**—the security (usually property) used to ensure payment of the loan; may include the physical address of the property
- **Credit Limit**—the highest amount you can use on this account
- **Past Due**—the amount overdue on the account
- **Terms**—the total payments you agreed to pay on the repayment plan
- **Payment Status**—indicates if you have paid, late paid, or are past due on the account
- **Account Type**—additional details about the type of account
- **Responsibility**—lists who signed to repay the loan (individual or joint)
- **Date Opened**—when the account was opened
- **Date Closed**—when the account was closed
- **Date Paid**—when the loan was paid off in full

How to Get a Copy of Your Credit Report

To thoroughly repair your credit, you must review a credit report from each of the three major credit bureaus since information will vary between reports, as will the credit score provided by each agency. The good news is you are entitled to one free credit report from each of the three agencies each year. You are also entitled to an additional free report from each of the bureaus if:

- You were denied credit within the last 60 days

- You are unemployed and attempting to find employment within the next 60 days
- You are on welfare
- You are a victim of fraud or identity theft (and have filed a police report)

You can request your free credit reports via telephone, the Internet (annualcreditreport.com), or snail mail (see the Appendix for a template). The information you need to provide to verify your identity and qualify to receive your credit report varies from one bureau to the next, but in most cases you will be asked for your:

- Social security number
- Creditor information
- Former addresses (and the dates you lived at each location)
- Employment history

Following is the contact information for each of the credit bureaus:

Equifax
Post Office Box 740241
Atlanta, GA 30374
(Their telephone number changes frequently. The current telephone number will be listed on your credit report.)
www.equifax.com

Experian

Post Office Box 2104

Allen, TX 75013-2104

888.397.3742

www.experian.com

TransUnion

2 Baldwin Place

Post Office Box 1000

Chester, PA 19022

800.916.8800

www.transunion.com

To make obtaining your credit information easier there is also a central source where you can obtain your free annual credit report from all three bureaus:

Annual Credit Report Request Service

Post Office Box 105281

Atlanta, GA 30348-5281

877.322.8228

www.annualcreditreport.com

Chapter Twelve
Removing Negative Records

What Can You Dispute?

The Fair Credit Report Act (FCRA) defines a process you can follow to dispute inaccurate or outdated tradelines and have them removed from your credit report. The FCRA is not intended to allow you to remove legitimate negative tradelines. In fact, the Credit Repair Organizations Act, which regulates the credit repair industry, requires credit repair companies to make the following disclaimer to their clients:

> *You have a right to dispute inaccurate information in your credit report by contacting the credit bureau directly. However, neither you nor any "credit repair" company or credit repair organization has the right to have accurate, current, and verifiable information removed from your credit report. The credit bureau must remove accurate, negative information from your report only if it is over 7 years old. Bankruptcy information can be reported for 10 years.*

However, even if a negative item on your credit report is yours, it may not be reported accurately or be verifiable in a timely manner. And that's good news for you because, if a negative tradeline on your report contains *any* errors (such as incorrect number of days late or amount of your current balance) or omissions (like missing account information), you can initiate a dispute. If the credit bureau is unable to verify or update the information within 30 days, the entire entry must be removed from your credit file!

Finding Errors and Omissions

Research shows that approximately 80% of all credit reports
include errors. Based on my experience in the industry, I feel that
estimate is actually on the low side. Given all of the information
that a single entry should accurately report, there are many
opportunities for a creditor to make an error (see the section
entitled What is Included in Your Credit Report for a complete list).
All you need to find is a single error on an entry to initiate a
dispute. In actuality, you can initiate a dispute even if you don't find
a reporting error or omission at all! More on that later.

Here's what to look for when reviewing your credit report for errors
and omissions:

1. Ensure your name is spelled correctly and that only
    one name appears on your report. If you're a Jr. or II
    it's easy for the credit bureaus to receive information
    that actually belongs on Sr.'s or III's report and not
    yours. Names are also frequently misspelled (like
    'Smith' instead of 'Smyth'). Too many misspelled
    names on your account can cause creditors to be
    concerned that you may be using aliases to escape a
    bad credit history, or worse.

    To remove erroneous names or variations of your
    name that may appear in your credit file, simply send
    a letter requesting the update, along with copies of
    your valid driver's license and signed social security
    card, to the credit bureau asking them to update their
    records with your current legal name.

If you have legally changed your name for professional or personal reasons (marriage, for example) and there is bad credit associated with your previous name, you might consider having the old name removed from your credit file using the method described above. This strategy can make it more difficult for the credit bureaus to verify negative accounts associated with your former name. Before you remove a previous name, however, try to make sure that all of your positive accounts are reflected on your credit reports. Not all creditors report to all three bureaus, but if you notice any omissions of positive entries, contact the creditor and ask them to update your credit report before removing an old name.

2. Check that your Social Security number and birth date are correct. The last thing you want is someone else's credit history associated with your credit file.

3. Make sure your address(es) are correct. Incorrect addresses can lead to incorrect information in your credit file.

4. See if there are any accounts listed that are not yours. If you have never done business with a bank or store listed on your report, either someone else's credit erroneously ended up in your file because of a misspelled name or incorrect Social Security number, or worse, your identity may have been stolen and someone is using your information and credit.

5. Identify the accounts that list negative activity and review those accounts in detail for any missing or inaccurate information you can dispute.

6. Look for any account balance histories that are not up to date. Check to see whether a lender has updated the status of a negative account to reflect recent positive activity.

7. Search for any duplicate accounts (especially collection accounts). Accounts may be duplicated when a lender issues different types of credit accounts, like revolving and installment accounts, or when you change addresses and the creditor incorrectly creates a second account number associated with your new address even though you really only have one account.

8. Often you will find duplicate listings for collection accounts. When a lender writes off a non-collectable debt, they sell the account to a debt collector. Both the charge-off account and the collection account will be listed on your credit report. However, *if the collection agency that purchased your debt then sells the account to another collection agency, only the latest collection agency account should appear in the file; the older one should be removed.*

One exception, however, is a student loan. Student loans are often reported more than once on your credit file because each loan is reported as a separate loan for each enrollment period, such as each semester or year you were in college.

9. Determine if any discharged debts are reported as charge-offs. In a bankruptcy, when debts are discharged the debt balance becomes zero. The credit report entry should indicate the debt was discharged under the bankruptcy chapter. If a discharged debt is recorded as a charge-off it should be removed and/or updated.

10. Look for any closed overdraft protection accounts. Lines of credit established as overdraft protection accounts are sometimes reported to the credit bureaus. If the account for which the line of credit was established to protect has been closed, this data should be completely removed from your credit file. Obviously, this kind of account can remain if it is a positive account.

11. Search for any debt that is the responsibility of an ex-spouse. If you incur debt from a joint account held during a marriage, the data will appear on both spouses' credit reports. After a divorce, the original debt will still appear on both parties' credit files. However, any debt that is acquired individually by an ex-spouse during divorce proceedings should only appear on that person's credit report.

12. Review all the positive accounts and determine if any are missing. Make a list of any missing accounts you would like to have added to your report to help boost your credit score.

13. Compare each of your three credit reports. Make note of accounts that do not have matching

information on all reports. Also note any accounts listed on one of your credit files that are missing from one or more of the other reports. You can choose to dispute these non-matching and/or missing accounts.

The Dispute Process

As you know, the FCRA law allows you to dispute any information on your credit report that is outdated, inaccurate, or incomplete. When you file a dispute to help with credit repair, the credit bureaus are required to conduct an investigation and report the results of that investigation in a timely and appropriate manner.

There is absolutely no charge for this service—it's your right as a credit consumer.

You may file a credit report dispute online, over the telephone, or by mail (see the Appendix or Resource Library at DebtClear.com for letter templates). It is best to do everything in writing to create a document trail you can reference in case something goes wrong or gets lost. (You'll also get better results by submitting written requests for several more reasons I will describe in more detail below.) Send your letter by certified mail, return-receipt requested, so you can document that your dispute letter was mailed and when it was received. Always keep a photocopy of your dispute letter and any enclosures.

After you submit your dispute, the credit bureau will then contact the creditor who reported the disputed information. When the creditor receives a request for verification from the credit bureau, it must investigate the data, review all relevant information provided, and report the results of that investigation to the credit-reporting agency.

The credit bureau has 30 days to complete its investigation and another 7 days to notify you of the results. That's why you send dispute letters return-receipt requested: when the dispute letter is received, the clock starts ticking. *If the credit bureau does not complete its investigation and notify you within 37 days of receiving your dispute—regardless of whether the entry is in fact valid—the entry must be removed from your credit file.*

If the investigation and notification is completed within the required timeframe, your results will be one of the following:

1. No change, along with a reason why the item is unchanged
2. Updated, with new information
3. Deleted (Yes!)

The credit bureau will also provide you with a free copy of your updated credit report if the dispute results in a change to your credit report.

If an entry is in any way changed or removed, the credit bureau is not allowed to put the information back on your report unless the creditor who provided the information later verifies its accuracy. In that case, the credit bureau is required to notify you, in writing, that the disputed data is being put back on your credit report (keep in mind, this rarely happens). They must also provide you with the name, address, and phone number of the company that submitted the verification.

You may also request that the credit bureau send notices of the corrections to anyone who reviewed your credit report within the last six months.

Chapter Thirteen
Dispute Strategies

Disputing Primary Creditor Records

To initiate a dispute, send a letter of dispute to the credit-reporting agency (see the Appendix or the Resource Library at DebtClear.com for a template).

Written requests for an investigation should:

1. Explain why you are disputing the item(s)

2. Request an investigation to resolve the issue, including the contact information of any furnisher of information

3. Include a copy of the credit file with the disputed entries circled

4. Include a copy of your driver's license and current utility bill to verify your identity

5. Include any additional supporting documentation coded to match the entries circled on the credit report

If you have accounts that do not reflect the same information on each of your three credit reports you can request that the two reports be made to match. For example, if your TransUnion file states that your Citibank account is 60 days late, but your Experian file reports the same account is 90 days late, you can send a copy of the TransUnion credit report to Experian along with a request stating you want the account to be reported as 60 days late.

If the credit bureaus fail to provide full report details on any account, each omission is considered a reporting error and the negative entry must be updated or removed. If, say, your Experian credit report lists a negative account while your TransUnion report shows no entry for that account, you can dispute the negative account by sending Experian a copy of your TransUnion report and request the negative account be removed because it is inaccurate.

Disputing Charge-Off Records

After 180 days of non-payment, an original creditor usually charges off a delinquent account and records it as a loss on its books. The lender then sells or assigns the uncollectible debt—uncollectible to the original creditor, anyway—to a debt collector who will then try to collect the debt from you.

The original creditor may write the debt off its books, but that does not mean the account is written off your credit file. In fact, a charge-off is considered a serious negative entry on your report—much more serious than, say, a late payment.

Strategies for removing a charge-off from your credit report include:

1. Check for any inaccurate dates, amounts, or missing information that should be listed. The balance of a charge-off account should be listed as zero. The account must list the charge-off date, the write-off

date, the first date of delinquency, and the date of removal.

2. Ensure account dates are correct, such as the date of the first delinquency and the date the bad credit is expected to be removed from the file.

3. Request a charge-off statement from the creditor. If they cannot supply a statement, the charge-off is considered to be invalid and must be removed.

Removing Remarks

The credit bureaus allow the consumer to include comments for each disputed account. However, they also allow the lender to include a comment in response to the consumer's remark, such as, "While consumer disputes information, data is verified as accurate." Comments in general can hurt your chances for receiving credit. Your best bet is to avoid including remarks for individually disputed items.

If a lender inserts a comment, request that the credit bureau remove it. Also keep in mind notations made by a credit counseling company carries serious weight, falling somewhere between the effects of a foreclosure and a bankruptcy. Therefore, always try to have these removed, or try to prevent them from being put there in the first place.

Disputing Third-Party (Debt Collectors) Records

As you already know from reading the Debt Relief section of this book, third-party records are accounts that have been written off and sold or assigned by the primary lender to a debt collector after the account was considered uncollectible.

Disputing collection accounts is an effective credit repair strategy since many debt collectors are unable to produce the information required to verify an account. When they fail to verify an account, the entire entry must be removed from your credit file.

Remember the dunning letter? After you receive it (or its verbal equivalent) you have 30 days to dispute the debt, otherwise it is deemed valid. If you receive a dunning letter, always send a verification and validation letter (see the Appendix or the Resource Library at DebtClear.com) to the collector requesting verification of the account. Unless or until the debt is verified, the debt collector is not allowed to continue collecting efforts nor can they report the debt on your credit report.

If the debt collector continues to list the debt on your credit report, you can report them to the Federal Trade Commission and the Attorney General, as well as threaten to sue or sue them under the Fair Debt Collection Practices Act. Your goal is to have them stop collection and reporting activities because of their default on your verification request. Most likely, the collection agency will not be able to verify all of the required information and will sell it to another debt collector. You will need to repeat your dispute each time the account is sold to another collector, but that's okay. You now know how.

If you send a debt validation request after the 30-day validation period ends, the debt collector isn't legally required to respond to your request or stop collection activity on the account. That said, I have never known of a debt collector sending validation notices using any type of delivery confirmation. Since they don't have delivery confirmation, they cannot prove whether you actually received the validation.

Tip: If it has been more than 30 days since you received your dunning letter, or you never received one in the first place, try sending the Debt Validation Request For 30+ Days After Dunning Letter found in the Appendix or in the Resource Library at DebtClear.com. Send your validation request to a debt collector already reporting a negative to your credit report. Wait until you get your delivery confirmation return receipt back and then try disputing the negative *online* or *over the phone* with each credit bureau. Because debt collectors are required by law to not report negatives to the credit bureaus until they provide you with verification, many debt collectors (even if it has been more than 30 days since your dunning notification) will put your account in a non-reporting status until they provide validation. Initiating a dispute during this time may mean the entry is no longer verifiable and will be deleted from your report!

Time-Barred Debts

As you learned in the Debt Relief section, each state has a statute of limitations on debt collection. After a certain amount of time an unpaid, outstanding debt is no longer collectable and is considered a time-barred debt. If you have a time-barred debt still reporting on your credit report:

> 1. Verify the debt is time-barred by reviewing the statute of limitations chart below and verifying the

date of your last payment. In some states, the clock starts ticking on the date of your first missed payment while in others, it starts on the date of charge-off.

2. Consider contacting the creditor and offering a settlement to remove the record from your report, or to update the entry as "paid as agreed." But be careful since making even a partial payment can reset the statute of limitations on your debt! In no way—verbally or in writing—should you admit the debt is yours. In fact, take the opposite position. State that although you dispute the validity of the debt, and have no previous agreement or contract with the debt collector, you may be willing to enter into an agreement that in exchange for $X they agree to remove the record from your report or have it updated to "paid as agreed". But never, ever admit the debt is in fact yours. (For more information see the Settlement Tutorial in the Roadmap section of this book or at DebtClear.com.)

3. Also, check your credit reports carefully. If your collection account has passed the statute of limitations you have the right to sue a collection agency for pulling your credit report for review. The threat of this suit could also be used as a bargaining chip to have the record removed or updated.

Debt Collection Statute of Limitations by State

Alabama	3 years
Alaska	3 years
Arizona	3 years
Arkansas	5 years (2 years for medical debt)
California	4 years
Colorado	6 years
Connecticut	6 years
Delaware	3 years
District of Columbia	3 years
Florida	5 years
Georgia	4 years
Hawaii	6 years
Idaho	5 years
Illinois	10 years
Indiana	6 years
Iowa	5 years
Kansas	5 years

Kentucky	5 years
Louisiana	3 years
Maine	6 years
Maryland	3 years
Massachusetts	6 years
Michigan	6 years
Minnesota	6 years
Mississippi	3 years
Missouri	5 years
Montana	8 years
Nebraska	4 years
Nevada	4 years
New Hampshire	3 years
New Jersey	6 years
New Mexico	4 years
New York	6 years
North Carolina	3 years
North Dakota	6 years

Ohio	6 years
Oklahoma	3 years
Oregon	6 years
Pennsylvania	4 years
Rhode Island	10 years
South Carolina	3 years
South Dakota	6 years
Tennessee	6 years
Texas	4 years
Utah	4 years
Virginia	3 years
Vermont	3 years
Washington	6 years
West Virginia	5 years
Wisconsin	6 years
Wyoming	8 years

Disputing Medical Records

Most hospitals and physicians do not report your payment history to the credit bureaus, mainly because they wish to avoid paying fees for reporting payment histories. But, if an uncollectible medical debt is sold to a debt collector, the account will most likely end up reported in your credit history.

The good news is medical debt is easy to dispute. Why? Due to medical insurance fraud, the law requires that specific information be maintained to prove a claim is legitimate. Since many collection agencies do not have the information required, they will be unable to verify the debt and the entry must be removed from your credit file. Ask the collection agency to provide a copy of your driver's license. If a collection agency or a medical provider can't prove your identity, you can claim the charge is not yours.

Strategies for Removing a Bankruptcy Record

A bankruptcy record is the most damaging form of bad credit; having a bankruptcy listed in your credit file will destroy your credit score. Worse yet, Chapter 7 bankruptcies remain on your file for 10 very long years. The following is a two-part tactic you can try to have a bankruptcy record removed from your credit file.

The average person will have between 10 and 20 individual accounts included in their credit report's bankruptcy listing. The credit bureaus refer to the listed accounts as the "tracks" of a bankruptcy. When a credit bureau runs a bankruptcy verification request through its automated system, the system pulls only one of the "tracks" in order to verify that the bankruptcy record is legitimate and should remain in the file. But what if the "track" the system pulls is missing? The system reports that the bankruptcy is not verifiable and it is removed from the credit report!

Therefore, the strategy here is to remove as many of those "tracks" as you can from your credit reports *first,* before you dispute the bankruptcy itself. The more tracks you can remove, the greater your odds of successfully removing the bankruptcy.

How do you remove "tracks"? Follow the same process as for disputing inaccurate or incomplete information from any other account. For example, compare your three reports. If a "track" is listed on one report but is missing from another, you can dispute whether it should be listed at all by sending the credit bureau a copy of the report on which it is not listed.

Once you have removed as many tracks as you feel you can, dispute the bankruptcy itself. Just like any other account, if bankruptcy data is inaccurate or incomplete you can dispute it. The following information must be included with a bankruptcy listing:

- All lender accounts associated with the bankruptcy
- The bankruptcy filing date
- The bankruptcy date of discharge
- The bankruptcy attorney's name

First, dispute the bankruptcy itself. If it is verified, you can file additional disputes based on any of the above reasons. Remember to submit documentation to support additional disputes, otherwise the bureaus might consider your dispute frivolous and not re-investigate. The more times they re-investigate, the greater the odds that they will use one of the tracks you have deleted to verify the bankruptcy, and it will be deleted.

Avoiding Frivolous Disputes

The credit bureaus are required by law to investigate a dispute unless they consider your request frivolous. If a credit bureau does determine that your request is frivolous, they are required to notify you within five business days and:

1. Tell you why your request is considered frivolous, and
2. Explain what you can do to convert the frivolous dispute into a legitimate request that will result in an investigation.

If you send a laundry list of disputes to the credit bureau, it can appear that your strategy is simply to dispute all the negatives on your report, which isn't the intended purpose of the dispute process. The dispute process established by the FCRA is intended to update or remove inaccurate or outdated information from your credit report. If you dispute every negative entry at once, it looks like you are just trying to remove negatives from your report, regardless of whether they are valid or not. However, the FCRA states that the credit bureaus can deny your requests for this very reason!

To avoid the appearance of making frivolous requests, include one to three disputes per request letter, and space out your requests over six to eight weeks. This way you will stay under their "frivolous dispute" radar.

If you need to dispute an account that has already been investigated and verified, *you must dispute the account for a different reason*. For example, if your initial request disputed the high credit amount on a specific account, your next request might dispute the amount past due on that account. Remember to always supply supporting documentation if you have it.

TIP: Often waiting 3 months or so before submitting another dispute on a tradeline already verified is enough to have another investigation performed. Requests deemed frivolous will come back as "previously verified."

If they continue to deny your valid reinvestigation requests, you may threaten to file a complaint with the Federal Trade Commission and with their state's Attorney General. If it comes to this, see the section below on What to Do if the Credit Reporting Agency is Unresponsive for further instructions.

Avoiding the Credit Bureau's Automated System

Working outside the automated system is perhaps the single most important technique you can use for credit repair. Credit reporting agencies receive approximately 10,000 disputes per day! That's a lot of investigations they need to conduct. How do the credit bureaus handle the onslaught of disputes? They use an automated system to receive *and* investigate disputes. If your dispute gets picked up by the automated system, you'll probably receive an automatic confirmation verifying that the information is correct; no actual investigation occurred and no corrections will be made to your file. The automated system is a "reconfirmation" system, rather than a "reinvestigation" system.

The key is to have a person receive and investigate your dispute letter; that way not only does an actual investigation occur, but mistakes could be made because people make mistakes.

To make sure you avoid the automated dispute processing system:

1. Dispute everything in writing. Do not dispute items by phone or online.

2. Make a clerical error (or errors) in your letter, like adding an extra digit to your address, tossing in a punctuation sign in the middle of your Social Security number, or intentionally misspelling a few words.

3. Or, simply handwrite your dispute letter. Just make sure it is legible.

4. Cite sections, titles, and codes of the law in your letter (already contained in our letter templates).

5. Ask for the name and address of the person who verified the account, along with the method they used to verify the account.

Remember the bureaus have to respond in a timely *and* appropriate manner. By avoiding the automated dispute process and requesting the additional information contained in our letter templates, you are increasing the likelihood that the bureaus won't be able to respond in time (within 37 days), or that their response will be inadequate. Either scenario gives you leverage to have the record removed.

Making a Settlement Offer

Another strategy for removing negatives from your credit report is to reach a settlement agreement with your creditor. If you decide to settle on an account you should always include as part of the settlement agreement that they must:

1. Remove the tradeline from your credit report, or update your account status to "paid as agreed", and

2. Stop reporting the collection account to the credit bureaus.

If your account has been sold to a debt-buyer, they may not be able to update your original creditor record. If your account was assigned to a debt collector, you should be able to update the original creditor file and delete any associated collection accounts. *Remember to always get everything in writing prior to paying them.* Please review the section on Settlements if you want to go this route and remember:

1. Never concede the debt is your account or responsibility.

2. Any associated collection account(s) must be removed from each of your credit files.

3. The original account must reflect a zero balance and be listed as "paid as agreed" (if creditor is still the original creditor).

4. All collection proceedings must stop and the creditor or debt collector has no right to legally pursue the debt any further or to sell/transfer the account.

Remember, the difference between the amount you owe on a debt and the amount you actually pay in a settlement is considered by the IRS as taxable income. The creditor or debt collector is required by law to report to the IRS, using form 1099, the amount of money forgiven in the settlement, and you may be responsible to pay taxes on that amount. I use the word "may" because reporting doesn't always occur. In fact, most of the time it doesn't (people receive a 1099 less than 20% of the time). However, negotiating over 1099 reporting is something you should never do. Don't even make the request. Never ask that your account with the original creditor be updated as "paid in full", either. In both cases you are requesting—in writing—that they break the law.

Always keep in mind tax implications if you are considering settling. Settling a $10,000 debt for $1,000 just to get it off your credit report might mean you are paying several thousand dollars more in taxes down the road. If you have the time, consider waiting until the statue of limitations expires on the debt. Creditors are much less likely to report on time-barred debts, so initiating a dispute after the statute of limitations has expired is likely to result in its removal.

To Add or Not To Add a 100 Word Statement

You are allowed to add a 100-word statement to your credit file to explain any negative information, or to dispute data you believe to be inaccurate and that the credit bureau will not remove from your record. A 100-word statement will not change your credit score, but it may help lenders or employers who check your credit report make a more informed decision.

Does a 100-word statement help? The answer depends on who reviews your statement and what you write. Some creditors will never read a statement, while other lenders may read it and ask you to verify the information you wrote as part of the process of considering your application.

Think of it this way: the only way a 100-word statement can hurt is if it remains on your file and becomes outdated. If you place a statement in your credit report and several months later the account is no longer delinquent and instead reflects a recent positive payment history, your old statement will only serve to highlight a past negative situation.

TransUnion offers assistance with writing your 100-word statement. Call 800-916-8800 for help.

What to Do if the Credit Reporting Agency is Unresponsive

If you have appropriately and diligently disputed an item and the credit bureau fails to notify you of the results of a dispute, re-investigate a dispute, or remove negative information from your file that was confirmed to be inaccurate, incomplete, or outdated, there are steps you can take and resources you can use to deal with the problem.

If the credit bureau fails to remove or correct the inaccurate, outdated, or unverifiable information within 30 days (you should receive investigation results within 37 days of their receipt of your dispute), you should send the letter Credit Bureau Failure to Respond in 37 Days found in the Appendix or in the Resource Library at DebtClear.com.

As you can see, this letter is not a request for re-investigation, but a demand that they remove the negative from your report due to their failure to respond in a timely or appropriate manner. It gives them 30 days to comply or else you will file complaints with the Federal Trade Commission, their state's Attorney General, and you will pursue legal action.

You can file a complaint online with the Federal Trade Commission at www.ftc.gov. After filing the complaint you will get a dispute number. Next, send a formal letter of complaint to the Federal Trade Commission along with copies of evidence that the bureau failed to respond to your dispute, yet is still reporting the disputed item.

Federal Trade Commission
Consumer Response Center
600 Pennsylvania Avenue, NW
Washington, DC 20580
Telephone: 877.382.4357

You should receive a response from the Federal Trade Commission within 15 to 30 days. If the FTC findings favor your position, send another letter to the bureau demanding that the item be removed along with a copy of the FTC letter.

If that still doesn't do the trick, you might consider getting legal representation and actually suing. The law allows you to recover attorney's costs and legal fees as well as any excess interest you paid creditors based on increased interest rates caused by the negative information remaining in your file. You may also recover punitive damages if the court finds the credit bureau acted willfully and intentionally in not correcting or removing the negative information.

To locate an attorney experienced in consumer credit issues, check out the National Association of Consumer Advocates at www.naca.net, or visit DebtClear.com for a referral.

Chapter Fourteen
Credit Building Strategies

So far we have talked a lot about removing negative items from your credit report to help with credit repair. However, credit repair is a two-part process: 1) removing negative entries from your report that pull your score down, and 2) employing a number of other strategies to help *build up* your credit score.

15 Tips for Building Credit & Improving Your Credit Score

1. **Add Positive Accounts to Your File**. If you have accounts in good standing that do not appear on your credit file, your goal is to have them included. Not all creditors report to all agencies since it costs money to do so. If you see a positive account that does not appear on one of your reports, contact the creditor and ask them to report to that bureau. You can't contact the credit bureau and ask them to verify positive information; they only handle disputes over negative records. Therefore, supplying a bureau with evidence that a positive entry is on another report will not cause that bureau to add the entry. Bureaus must be notified by the creditors themselves regarding positive accounts. While lenders are not required to report your credit to all three bureaus, they might do so for a fee that covers their reporting costs. If adding the account to a report will improve your credit rating, it could be well worth the cost. Just

contact the creditor not reporting a positive account and ask.

2. **Keep Your Oldest Accounts Open and Current**. If you are finding that you can no longer service your debt on all of your accounts and you are trying to decide which accounts to default on, one strategy is to default on the account(s) you have opened most recently. The reason is that the older your active accounts are, the more positive impact they have on your credit score.

3. **Get Up To Date, and Stay Current on Any Missed or Late Payments.** Recent activity has a greater effect on your credit rating than older activity (for example, making a late payment on your car loan can drop your credit score by more than 100 points for as long as three months). Therefore, one way to improve your score is to get current and stay current on those accounts you can afford to pay on. The longer you pay your bills on time, the better your credit score. Whenever possible, set up automatic payments to ensure timely and consistent payments.

4. **Do Not Use More Than 30%-50% of Your Credit Limit.** To ensure maximization of your credit score you should use no more than 30 – 50% of the credit limit on your credit cards. If your credit limit is $1,000, don't use more than $500 for purchases, and try to keep your balance below $300.

5. **Don't Pay Your Balances Off Every Month.** Part of your score is your credit worthiness, but part of it

also indicates how desirable (read "profitable") you are to a creditor. If you pay off the balances on your credit cards every month, then the credit card company doesn't get to charge you any interest. Though the actual percentage isn't known, you want to keep your balances somewhere between 0% and 30% of your credit limit to receive the maximum bump in your credit score.

6. **Don't Move Debt Around.** Transferring balances from one credit card to another to save a few points on your interest rate will cost you more than you realize—and the cost will be reflected in a lowered credit score.

7. **Apply For and Open New Credit Accounts Only As Needed.** New accounts lower your average account age; a lower average account age can have a dramatic effect on your credit score. Plus, rapid account "buildup" makes you seem like a greater credit risk, lowering your credit rating. Apply for and open new accounts (as well as request credit increases on already established accounts) only when you need to.

8. **Build Credit with Everyday Purchases.** If you pay your cable bill or grocery bill by check or debit card, consider making these payments with a credit card and then paying off the card. Yes, it is an extra step, but paying your cable bill on time each month by check is not going to build your credit. Remember,

every on-time credit card payment helps raise your credit score.

9. **Diversify Your Credit.** An important goal is to develop a mix of different types of credit in order to show you are capable of balancing different repayment obligations for credit cards, retail accounts, installment loans, consumer finance accounts, etc. Of all the different types of credit, installment accounts like mortgage or auto loans will help improve your score the most. One store or gas card, one credit card, a mortgage and an auto loan is probably the best mix of credit. Try to stay away from financing companies (as opposed to banks) as these types of loans can actually hurt your score.

10. **Use a Major Purchase To Boost Your Credit Score.** Making an expensive, large-ticket item purchase like a home or a car will greatly increase your credit rating because: (a) the loan is secured with collateral (the safest type of loan), and (b) the loan payment is the same each month, allowing the credit bureaus to measure how you handle making a fixed payment every month.

11. **Use Retail Cards.** Retail cards, also called store cards, can be a great way to establish or build credit. Store cards are similar to credit cards, except they can only be used to make purchases at the store that issued you the card. Store cards are easier to get than standard credit cards, but they tend to carry much higher interest rates. If you get a store card,

use it only for small purchases you can pay down each month; that way you don't get charged high interest, but you are still able to build a solid credit history by making payments on time. Make sure the retailer reports the information to one or more of the main credit bureaus. If they don't, ask them to do so. If they will not, find a store that does.

12. **Consolidate Student Loans.** A good student loan strategy is to consolidate them after graduation. You can usually refinance all your individual loans into a single loan at a lower interest rate and on longer payment terms. After consolidation, all the individual student loans on your credit report will be reported as closed and paid in full, helping to improve your credit rating. A consolidated loan also allows you to change your payment plans based on your current income. Make sure to set up a payment plan that works best for you, since a student loan remains on your credit report until paid in full. Student loans are not written off or discharged in bankruptcy, and since most student loans are guaranteed by the government, if you fail to make your payments it is easy for Uncle Sam to hold back tax refunds or garnish wages.

13. **Consider a Cosigner.** If you have trouble getting credit, consider having another person with better credit co-sign for the loan. To a lender, having a co-signer means you and the co-signer are both liable for re-paying the loan, even if you are the only one who will actually make payments. Over time, if you maintain a positive payment history on the account,

your credit score will improve. But, if you should default on the loan, your cosigner's credit will be adversely affected, so make sure you can consistently pay on time.

14. **Obtain a Secured Card.** If you don't qualify for a standard credit card account, you can get a secured card to help build your credit. A secured credit card requires you to deposit your own funds (equal to the secured card's credit limit) in an account to guarantee payment for purchases you make using the card. The account is reported to the credit bureaus and you make payments on the account just like you would a regular credit card. If you fail to make a payment the lender will pull the payment from your deposited funds. If you make all your payments on time, in about a year or so you should be able to qualify for an unsecured credit card. Keep in mind some creditors may try to take advantage of your inability to acquire a standard credit card by offering you a secured card that comes with an annual fee and monthly processing fees. You should not have to pay fees to obtain a secured card. Shop around until you find a bank or credit union that does not charge a fee or fees for granting you a secured card. Or just visit DebtClear.com for a referral.

15. **Use a Savings Account or Equity in Your Home to Borrow Your Own Money.** If you have a checking account at a bank, you can open a savings account and then use the savings account as collateral to take out a small loan the bank will report

to the credit bureaus. As you pay back the loan you create a positive credit history. You'll be on your way to building your credit in a short period of time. If you have equity in your home you can take out a home equity loan and use your on-time payments to build up your credit. Be careful, however, because unlike secured debt, this loan is secured by your home.

Credit Strategies for Purchasing a Home

If you plan to purchase a home, make sure your credit file is in as good shape as possible. The FHA requires all three of your credit reports to be reviewed to determine your credit risk before it will approve a mortgage. The best strategy to increase your credit rating is to clean up your credit file, get all your accounts current, and pay down your debt prior to applying for a home loan.

To qualify for a home loan:

1. You typically must have a combined credit score (the average of the three credit bureau scores) of 620 or higher.

2. You cannot have outstanding delinquent debt on your credit file (unless it is more than five years old and less than $5,000).

3. Charge-offs cannot be less than 3 years old.

4. Judgments must be paid off.

5. You cannot have too much open credit.

6. You cannot have too much new credit in the last year.

7. You should ideally have three types of credit: mortgage, credit card, and car loan. If you are a first-time homebuyer and do not have a mortgage loan history, the types of accounts in your credit file should be: a credit card (secured cards are acceptable but considered a higher risk), an auto loan or car lease (via a bank, not a financing company), and a retail store card (such as Sam's Club or Costco).

8. If you own your own business, your tax returns must report a profit for the previous two years.

9. There must be no record of late payments for any of your accounts for the last 6 months.

Urban Legend? I have been told (though I haven't independently verified it) that if you initiate a dispute with the bureaus and pull your credit file sometime during the investigation, the disputed information will not be factored into your overall score. If someone wants to try this and let us know if it works, I will post the results on the DebtClear.com blog.

In Conclusion

I know we covered a lot of information in this section. Remember, credit repair is a process and not an event. It takes time, diligence, organization, and, of course, an understanding of how the game is played. Here are some of the finer points to remember:

1. Regularly monitor your credit report with a 3-in-1 credit monitoring service.

2. Dispute negative tradelines individually, and no more than a few at a time.

3. Avoid the automated system by only sending dispute letters with errors that are hand written, etc.

4. Send all correspondence certified mail with return receipt.

5. If a credit bureau fails to respond in a timely or appropriate manner escalate the issue and demand removal.

6. If a disputed tradeline has already been verified, wait a few months and try again.

7. Add positive accounts to your reports and have the right mix of credit.

8. Keep balances low and pay on time.

Because of the amount of work and diligence credit repair requires, many choose to hire a credit repair service. *Be careful when shopping around*. Most companies out there do little but send out form letters every 45 days with generic dispute requests. For a list of credit repair and credit monitoring services we recommend, visit our website at DebtClear.com.

Creditor Lawsuits

Chapter Fifteen
Will You Be Sued?

First the bad news: some people receive debt collector lawsuits from creditors who are attempting to recover a debt. If that suit is successful for the collector, a judgment is entered, and the creditor can enforce that creditor lawsuit by garnishing wages, putting liens on property, and even taking money out of your bank account.

But here's the good news: in our experience, only about 20% of accounts receive lawsuits. In fact, one of our partners reports that only 6% of its clients are sued by original creditors or debt-buyers.

And here's the better news. Say you *are* sued: if you understand your rights, know how the system works, and get help when you need it, in most cases you can make it too difficult or expensive for the creditors to win and you may eventually get the case dropped.

Here's why.

98% of the time when a creditor sues a debtor, one of two things happens:

1. The debtor buries his or her head in the sand and doesn't respond to the lawsuit and the creditor gets a judgment by default; or

2. The debtor shows up in court and tells the judge some sad story about how they got into their present situation. However, all the judge cares about is whether the account is theirs and whether they made the charges. The debtor says, "Yes, but…" and the judge again rules in favor of the creditor.

Remember, suing someone is the most expensive collection effort a creditor can pursue. Even if they get a judgment, they still have to enforce that judgment and there is no guarantee they will be able to collect anything at the end of the day. As a group, those who can't make minimum payments to their creditors don't have a lot of assets to collect on.

Even the worst attorneys—and believe me, collection attorneys are the worst—still bill at least a couple hundred dollars per hour for their time.

So let's look at this from the creditor's perspective:

- They most likely purchased your account for pennies on the dollar.

- They are used to winning the vast majority of their lawsuits by default.

- Enforcing these judgments costs even more time and money with no guarantee for return.

As long as creditors are making money by suing debtors they will continue to do so.

However, if you know your rights and respond to the creditor lawsuit with requests for discovery (interrogatories, admissions, etc.), you throw a wrench in their business model. In order to pursue the suit, they have to keep spending more and more money and pretty soon their theoretical profit margin disappears and they start losing real money.

Furthermore, the more work you throw at these bottom-feeding collection attorneys, the more likely it is that they will mess up somehow, allowing you to have the case dismissed!

Let's start with original creditors. (An original creditor is the company that first offered you credit. For example, if you apply for and receive an HSBC credit card, HSBC is the original creditor.) Some original creditors are much more likely to sue in order to recover a debt than others. As you know, if you have not made a payment on a credit card debt for 180 days, the original creditor will discharge or write off that debt. The original creditor will then either assign the debt to a collector who collects on their behalf, or sell your account outright to a third-party debt collector—usually for around 10 cents on the dollar.

Whether the debt is assigned or sold actually makes a difference when it comes to a debt collection lawsuit. *That's because debt-buyers are less likely to have the supporting documentation you are going to demand they produce as part of the court proceedings.* Oftentimes, a debt-buyer—also known as a third-party debt collector—will simply purchase a database with your name, the account number, and how much you allegedly owe.

Notice the word *allegedly* in the previous sentence? "Allegedly" is an important concept you must understand when it comes to debt collection lawsuits. You are innocent until proven guilty. The burden of proof is on the creditor to prove that you owe them money, not for you to prove that you don't. They are the ones alleging that you owe them money. In responding to a creditor lawsuit you are in effect saying, "I am unsure whether or not I owe XYZ Collections any money. Therefore, I need XYZ collections Company to prove it to me and to the court." Otherwise, anyone could sue anybody for any reason and win!

Original creditors are a bit more tenacious when it comes to a debt collection lawsuit for a couple of reasons. First, they have access to all the information regarding your account, including your signed agreement and billing statements. Second, they have a lot more invested in your account. A third-party debt collector may have spent only 10 cents on the dollar for your account, while the original creditor is out almost the entire amount of the account.

While there are certainly no guarantees, and no way to accurately predict your likelihood of being sued by an original creditor, our experience—and the experience of our partners—does allow us to make a few assumptions:

- Citibank is fairly likely to file a creditor lawsuit to recover debt

- Discover is fairly likely to file a creditor lawsuit to recover debt

- Chase is very likely to file a creditor lawsuit [*]

- Credit unions are more likely to file a creditor lawsuit as well

On the other hand:

- Bank of America does not tend to file a creditor lawsuit to recover credit card debt

- Wells Fargo does not tend to file a creditor lawsuit

- HSBC does not tend to file a creditor lawsuit

- Companies who provide "store" cards underwritten by HSBC (like Target, Home Depot, etc.) do not tend to file a creditor lawsuit

Those original creditors less likely to sue tend to sell off their debts to debt-buyers. Some debt-buyers may eventually sue, but most won't for reasons already mentioned above.

On a related note: whether or not you'll be sued also sometimes depends—believe it or not—on where you live. You are more likely to be sued if you live in a major metropolitan area than if you live in a fairly isolated rural area. The reason is simple: big cities have more lawyers and law firms. For example, in Michigan, three major law firms tend to handle most debt litigation matters. In other states, like Wyoming, one firm gets the bulk of that work. So if you

---

[*] In the past Chase used the National Arbitration Forum (NAF) to win arbitrations and then have that result turned into a judgment. In July of 2009, however, the Attorney General of Minnesota forced the NAF to cease operations because of extensive financial ties that were found between the NAF and the debt collection industry. This may mean that we will see Chase suits drop dramatically in the future. Stay tuned.

stop making payments on multiple cards and you live in Michigan, it is likely that different firms would have to find and sue you; whereas, if you live in Wyoming, one firm may be serving you with multiple creditor lawsuits.

As a rule of thumb, if you live in a predominately rural state and you get one lawsuit, you're likely to get more. The flip-side is that, if you don't get one suit in a rural area, you probably won't get any.

Also keep in mind that if you receive a letter from a law firm threatening a creditor lawsuit, and that law firm is located outside your state, the odds are the letter is a bluff. In order to file a lawsuit, a law firm must be in your state. The law firm could choose to hire a local firm to pursue the debt litigation, but that doesn't happen particularly often.

Back to third-party debt collectors. Instead of suing right away, most start by playing a numbers game. They buy debts in bulk for pennies on the dollar and start by using the least expensive tactics possible to collect those debts—such as sending letters and making phone calls. Occasionally they ramp up their efforts by making threats, but in most cases they finally decide further effort isn't worth their trouble. As long as they collect on a certain percentage of the debts they buy, they're happy. They don't have to collect every debt in order to make a great living, they just need to collect on a certain percentage of the low-hanging fruit.

Once they decide further effort doesn't make sense, they sell your debt to another collector—or just stop trying altogether. Oh, they might send an occasional letter in hopes you'll finally cave, but most debt-buyers assume if they aren't successful within the first six to eighteen months or so, they might as well give up. It is simply a business reality of diminishing returns.

Eventually the statute of limitations runs out on the debt, and it is considered a time-barred debt and uncollectable by debt collection laws. If you were to receive a summons after your statute of limitations had expired, all you would need to do would be submit your state statute along with a copy of your credit report (showing the date of your last payment) to get the case dismissed.

So let's say you get a creditor lawsuit before your state's statute of limitations expires. What next?

Chapter Sixteen
An Overview of the Litigation Process

In later sections we'll look at how to prepare for the possibility of a lawsuit, and deal with that lawsuit if you are served. But first let's take a high-level look at the overall process, starting with the day you stopped making payments on a credit card. To keep things simple, we'll assume you have one credit card with a balance of $5,000.

You fall behind on your payments and your phone starts to ring. The calls start out as "friendly" reminders as they try to get you to make your account current. At this point they are fine with the fact that you are delinquent because they just added late fees to your account and maybe increased your interest rate as well.

If you continue to not pay, your phone will ring more frequently and the friendly reminders will start to turn into thinly veiled threats. If they can't get you to make your account current, they are going to try to get you to make a partial payment to reset the 180-day "clock." After 180 days of non-payment the credit card company usually writes off your debt. Remember, even making a partial payment can reset that time period.

They know the system, and they'll do anything possible to work the system to their advantage. But you know the system too. So you stand firm. After 4-5 months of non-payment, don't be surprised if you receive a settlement offer.

You should be aware that almost every original creditor or third-party debt collector will *threaten* to file a creditor lawsuit. The *threat* of a suit is a very inexpensive collection tactic and causes a large number of people to pay up. But a threat is just that—a threat.

While the debt collection laws say creditors cannot threaten to sue if they have no intention of suing, proving that they actually have no intention is tough and creditors know it. As long as a creditor occasionally sues a few people, they've shown they have some level of intent (after all, if I did it once, I might do it again). Don't let threats of a lawsuit intimidate you into paying. In most cases, the threat of a debt collection lawsuit is all bark and no bite.

If the original creditor chooses not to sue, they will assign or sell your debt to a debt collector. The debt collector then attempts to collect the debt, and around 20% of the time, you will receive a creditor lawsuit.

So let's assume a worst-case scenario, and a creditor decides to use litigation to collect the debt.

To file a debt collection lawsuit, a collection attorney draws up the necessary documents, pays a fee, and files those documents at your local civil courthouse. The court then requires the plaintiff (creditor) to "serve" you with a notice of that suit. That notice is called a "summons" because in effect you are "summoned" to appear at the court on a certain date and time. Service is required because, after all, if you don't know you are being sued how can you respond to that suit or mount a proper defense?

"Service" means different things in different jurisdictions. In the old days, service meant a person authorized by the court would personally hand you a summons. Now, depending on where you live you can be served in person, by certified mail, or by having the summons taped to your front door. (An easy way to find out how the process works in your area is to call your local courthouse and just ask how the summons process works.) In any case, the process cannot go forward until proper service, as defined in your jurisdiction, has occurred. That's why you see people running away from a process server in the movies—they're trying to avoid being served with a summons.

Summons and complaints are generally valid for approximately 45 days. (Again, the time period varies by locality so verify with your court.) If you aren't served within the statutory time period, the lawyer must re-file the suit, or simply let it go.

I know what you're thinking—if you don't get served properly you're home free, right?

Not necessarily. Oftentimes a debt collector will use improper service, or no service at all, as a technique to get a default judgment against you. Remember, if you don't respond to the summons you lose by default. Then you will need to go to the court and try to have the judgment lifted due to improper service, and eventually have to deal with the suit anyway. In my mind, if you receive a summons—even through improper service—it is probably better to just deal with the summons from the start.

That said, there is no reason to make legal service any easier for a creditor. There is no credit card debt law that says you have to sign for a certified letter, or answer your door, or identify yourself to a stranger.

Whether you respond to a suit that was improperly served is up to you. However, let's assume you were properly or improperly served and decided to respond.

Once you have been served you are given a specific amount of time to answer the complaint.

You must answer the complaint within the time frame specified on the summons or the creditor will get a default judgment against you.

And the judgment is almost always awarded for the full amount of the debt, plus interest, penalties, court fees.

Once that happens the game is over! You lost the suit, and they won. Without you even trying. *Doing nothing is absolutely the worst thing you can do.*

I briefly covered this above, but it bears repeating. Up until the point you are sued and a judgment is awarded, your debt is considered an *alleged* debt. The creditor alleges you owe a debt and it is up to the creditor to prove it. Don't make the creditor's job any easier by admitting to anything or handing them a default judgment.

When a creditor wins a suit, the law no longer sees the debt liability as alleged but as an actual debt. You lose your rights and they gain rights. They immediately get rights to place liens on your property, garnish wages, and levy (withdraw) money from your bank account.

That's why if you are sued, the worst thing you can do is ignore the suit. If you ignore the summons, the creditor automatically wins, ruining all the hard work you've done up to this point.

So go ahead and answer the complaint within the specified time period.

Answering the complaint isn't hard, but you will most likely need a little help and guidance (see the Resource Library at DebtClear.com). Your answer will force the creditor to provide information, and produce contracts and other documents proving you owe them money and that they have the right to collect on the alleged account.

The process you initiate by answering the complaint costs the creditor time and money. Calls are cheap. Letters are cheap. Threats are cheap. Creditor lawsuits are expensive, and responding to your requests for information is even more expensive.

By making the creditor prove the account is yours (how they calculated the amount of the alleged debt, that they are legally licensed to collect debts in your state, that they hold right, title, and interest in the debt, etc.) you put the burden of proof where it should be—on the creditor. The last thing you want to do is make their job any easier by saying to the judge, "Yes, the debt is mine but I lost my job and my wife died and my dog got sick…" You just proved the creditors case, so don't be surprised when the judge looks at you sympathetically and rules in the creditor's favor.

I am certainly not suggesting you should perjure yourself. All I am saying is there are no debt collection laws that say you need to make the creditor's case for them. You are the star witness and you can only make a conclusive determination (just like the court) based on the facts presented. I bet you don't have your account numbers memorized, or remember what purchases you made, or for how much, or even know whether the creditor suing you has a legal right to do so!

If Discover bank is your creditor and some other entity is trying to collect on the account, but they can't show any proof that they have a legal right to collect on the debt, then guess what? *They don't have a legal right to collect on the debt.* Whether you remember having a Discover card at one point and making some charges is immaterial.

The good news is that many debt-buyers don't respond to your requests for documentation (the part of the litigation process called discovery) for two reasons. First, as I already mentioned above, it is simply too costly. They are used to getting default judgments paying little more than a filing fee. Second, many debt collectors simply don't have the documentation required to respond to your discovery requests to prove their case.

If they don't prove their case in a timely or appropriate manner, you can move to have the case dismissed. And then you move on, too.

And if, after making them jump through all of these hoops, they are still pursuing you, you can always settle the account. Creditors don't want to go to trial anymore than you do. And if going to trial is what you want to do, our Lawsuit Defense Partner can help walk you through that process as well (visit DebtClear.com for more information). Chances are that, even if you get a judgment against you, the judge will lower the amount of the judgment which is also a victory in itself.

No matter what, you should take full advantage of your knowledge of the system, exercise your every right, and most of all never give up those rights.

That's the debt litigation process at a high level. Now let's look at the process in more detail. We'll start with what happens before a creditor lawsuit is filed.

Chapter Seventeen
Before a Lawsuit Is Filed

Defending yourself from litigation—or potential litigation—is based on three basic premises:

- **Protecting your assets** (see the chapter on Asset Protection) to minimize the impact if you are sued and a judgment is awarded.

- **Having affirmative defenses ready in case you are sued.** For example, you may have unresolved billing error disputes with the original creditor under the FCBA. Or you may have gathered FDCPA violations such as a failure to verify and validate the debt or calls you received after sending a Do Not Call letter, etc., that can be affirmative defenses.

- **Responding to a suit in a timely and appropriate manner and requesting discovery.**

Let's start with asset protection. Even if you are never sued, protecting your assets is still a smart move. Make sure you've done at least the basics: banking out of state, segregating accounts, and filing a homestead declaration (if applicable).

You can help lessen the impact of a judgment by taking smart asset protection steps now, while being aware of applicable fraudulent conveyance laws.

If you don't have any assets to protect in the first place and your income is exempt from collection, you have relatively little to fear from a lawsuit—at least not today. But since, depending on where you live, judgments are enforceable for periods ranging from three to twenty-five years, and may be renewable, you might have future assets to protect.

Next, there are some other proactive steps you can take that might provide affirmative defenses if a lawsuit ever comes down the pike. The first is billing error disputes.

Billing Error Disputes

Under the Fair Credit Billing Act, there are a number of reasons you can dispute an entry on a credit card bill. Here are a few of the most common:

- You didn't receive a statement
- The creditor failed to credit your account properly (payment, refund, etc.)
- You dispute a specific debit or charge

And a couple that are a bit more nebulous:

- An error of accounting (computation of finance charges, etc.)
- Clarification and verification of indebtedness (copy of the original agreement, signed credit card receipt, etc.)

Statement errors are easy to dispute, but are also easy for credit card companies to validate—the math is either right or wrong. Clarification and verification is a lot tougher. Merchants are required to maintain records of charge slips, but some merchants either fail to do so or fail to provide copies to the credit card companies upon request. If, for example, you ask for six months' worth of verification of charges, the credit card company is unlikely to be able to comply with your request. The credit card company has 30 days to provide verification, and 90 days total to resolve the dispute.

If your card account is under dispute, the creditor is not allowed to report your account as delinquent; they must report that the account is in dispute, which does not harm your credit. And while a debt liability is under dispute, you are not required to make a payment on that portion of your debt. After all, why should you *pay* when you might not actually *owe*? Keep in mind you can only stop paying for the debt that is in dispute; you cannot stop paying your entire bill. Unless you dispute everything on your bill, the credit card company can still report delinquencies on the part of your account that is not under dispute. Make sure you keep track of what is under dispute and what is not, and watch your credit report for inaccurate delinquency reporting.

But here's the key: *you have to file a bona fide dispute.* If you just pick up your statement and file a dispute saying, in effect, "I don't like the fact I owe this much money," you are wasting your time. Make sure you file a legitimate dispute. Ask for verification of a *particular charge.* Ask for validation of how interest or penalties were calculated. File a legitimate dispute that will stand up in court if you are sued.

Under the FCBA you have the right to dispute:

- Unauthorized charges (by law, liability for unauthorized credit card use is limited to $50; if your card is lost, stolen, etc., you are only liable for up to $50 of the unauthorized charges)

- Charges listing the wrong price or date of purchase

- Charges for items you did not receive or accept

- Math errors

- Payments not credited to your account or credited improperly

- Bills sent to the wrong address (if you send in a written change of address form within twenty days of when the billing cycle ends, bills should be sent to your new address)

Keep in mind that the FCBA will not cover disputes over price and for charges on items you don't want or that the store refuses to take back. The FCBA covers credit card errors, not disputes with the store or service provider.

The procedure to follow when filing a billing dispute depends upon your situation:

1. If you are current on your payments, you can dispute the most recent bill.

2. If you are not current, you must dispute a bill that was current within 60 days of that bill's receipt.

3. If you are over 60 days past due, you can either become current and go back to step 1, or decide not to dispute at all.

How do you file a billing dispute? Once you identify the specific items you wish to dispute:

1. Write a letter including your name, account number, date of the bill in dispute, a description of the item in dispute, and the reason why you think the bill is incorrect. Make a copy for your records. Then send your letter by certified mail, return receipt requested.

2. The credit company must respond acknowledging receipt of the dispute within thirty days of receiving your letter. Within 90 days they must investigate your dispute and render a decision. If you have requested a proof of purchase or other documentation, they must provide that documentation.

After you have received the response you can choose whether to continue the dispute or not. Write a letter within ten days, asking how they arrived at the decision and what information they used to make that decision.

Keep in mind that once 60 days has passed you cannot file a billing dispute.

If you plan to file a dispute, take a simple proactive step. Before you file, get a copy of your credit report. That way, if the creditor notes your account as delinquent rather than in dispute, you can use it to show damage to your credit as an affirmative defense if you receive a lawsuit (or as leverage to get the creditor to remove the entry from your credit report).

In many cases the credit card company will fail to respond. If they do respond, they might not provide sufficient information to resolve the dispute.

After 30 days, send a letter reminding the credit card company it has failed to address the dispute. Keep a copy for your records. Follow up again after 60 days.

After 90 days, check your credit report. See if the credit card company reported the account as disputed or delinquent. If it is reported as "delinquent," the credit card company is in violation of the Fair Credit Billing Act and you can use that as an affirmative defense if you are sued. If it is reported as "in dispute," you can use this as proof that the account was in dispute and you can show that it was not resolved.

Now that you understand the process, should you initiate a billing dispute?

As always, the choice is up to you. However, there is some anecdotal evidence to suggest that *filing billing error disputes may increase the likelihood that you will get a creditor lawsuit*, especially if you use a form letter the creditor has received in the past.

The thinking is this: if you have simply fallen behind on your payments and stopped answering your phone your creditors really don't know what is going on with you. You are part of the vast sea of delinquent accounts that they are trying to collect on and they are holding out hope that you will eventually pay.

However, filing a billing error dispute and then defaulting might signal to the original creditor that you are taking an offensive position and have no intent to pay. This strategy might make you stick out from the crowd. I personally think FCBA disputes are more trouble than they are worth, but, as always, the choice is yours.

FDCPA Violations

As you learned in the Debt Relief section, FDCPA violations are a much more likely occurrence and therefore a much better source of affirmative defenses against a creditor lawsuit.

For example, if a debt collector failed to respond appropriately to a verification and validation request, this is a great affirmative defense! The FDCPA states that ALL collection activities—including lawsuits—must stop until proper verification and validation has occurred. Since the language of what constitutes "proper verification" is somewhat ambiguous, you can usually assert that proper verification never occurred.

If you have been diligent in keeping a call log and documenting FDCPA violations, this log (along with any admissible telephone recordings you have) might also serve as a great affirmative defense.

It is important to note, however, that FBCA and FDCPA violations are violations of federal laws. Creditor lawsuits are civil actions. The difference is that civil courts don't have subject matter jurisdiction when it comes to federal laws. In other words, a civil court can't rule on federal issues, and federal courts can't rule on civil matters.

However, *if a federal suit is filed before a judgment is handed down in a related civil action, the federal suit trumps the civil suit.* Therefore, having documented FDCPA violations puts you in a powerful offensive position. The threat of a federal suit—or an actual pending suit filed before or during a civil action—can be a great way to get a creditor to back down or settle!

The last defensive strategy is to *make sure you respond to the lawsuit in a timely and appropriate manner.* Getting this first critical step wrong will give the creditors exactly what they want and expect—a quick and easy judgment against you.

So let's say you receive a creditor lawsuit. What next?

Chapter Eighteen
If a Lawsuit Is Filed

First things first: this is a long and relatively detailed chapter.

But don't worry, you don't have to memorize all the material, earn a law degree, or even play a lawyer on TV. My goal in this section is to make sure you understand the process and some of the steps you can take to defend yourself from creditors who file a lawsuit against you to recover a debt. Remember, the more hoops you make them jump through, the more likely they are to give up or mess up. For additional help, listen to the recorded tutorials in the DebtClear.com Resource Library and consider enrolling in our Lawsuit Defense Partner Program.

Of course, you can always hire an attorney who specializes in this area, but if the debt is yours, an attorney is most likely going to advise you to settle (that is, unless you have documented affirmative defenses). You may be able to go it alone with the help found in this book and on the DebtClear website, but you should consider enrolling in our Lawsuit Defense Partner Program—an educational membership organization that has been helping people like you defend themselves against creditor lawsuits for close to 10 years. They know all the players and their tricks and can teach you how to mount a proper defense. Visit DebtClear.com for more information.

Back to what to expect. Let's start with the summons.

As you know, if a creditor files a lawsuit against you, you must be notified of that lawsuit in the form of a summons. The summons is usually accompanied by a complaint generated by the plaintiff (the party doing the suing) and must be answered or else a default judgment will be entered against the defendant (you). Serving jail time is not a possibility—there is no debtor's jail!

We've talked about proper service, but the subject bears a little repetition. "Proper" service depends entirely on your state's laws. In Ohio, for example, the sheriff's department generally executes service. The collection attorney filing the suit goes to the courthouse, pays filing and service fees, files the lawsuit, and the court gives a service copy to the sheriff. The sheriff sends the Summons and Complaint out by certified mail; the same day he files a return of service saying he has served the summons, whether you receive it or not (ouch).

On the flip side, in Michigan if the summons is not placed in your hand, then you haven't been served. In Illinois, when you are served you'll find out a court date has already been set and you will have to appear.

Keep in mind the entire legal process cannot begin until you have been served. If you receive a card from the Post Office stating you have a certified letter that you must sign for but you do not respond, then you have not been served. Or, if you find a notice from the Sheriff's Department taped to your front door asking you to call because they have "important documents" they wish to give you, again, you do not have to respond and you haven't been served. There is no law that says you have to make it easy for a process server to present you with a summons for a creditor lawsuit.[11]

To find out how the process works in your state, check out the state and county rules in your locale. Find out what constitutes proper service, and what you are required to do once you *have* been served. Check with your state and county—or consult a local attorney—for the most updated information. We have also put together a list of special rules for each state at DebtClear.com for your reference.

Why? Because once you are served, you'll need to take action. **You must answer the complaint within the specified time period or you will lose by default.** The clock starts ticking on that time period usually the day after you have been served.

In every state there are things that must be done immediately. In Maryland, for example, you must file a Notice of Intent to Defend within 15 days and start the process of discovery within another 15 days.

Things can happen quickly, so don't delay and never, ever, just stick your head in the sand. Non-responsiveness is deemed an admission of guilt and you will lose 100% of the time. Go to the courthouse and file your response in person using the original documents; that way you'll be sure your response was received.

---

[11] Again, in some states the creditor need only make a *reasonable* effort to serve you before you are deemed served. Make sure you check your state's service laws.

Keep a copy of your response for your records, and also send a copy to the law firm listed on the complaint.

Because the rules vary so drastically by state, we recommend that you either hire an attorney or enroll with our Lawsuit Defense Partner Program immediately upon getting served. To get you started, however, we have compiled a list of state-specific information on our website. Alternatively, you can perform an Internet search for "yourstate civil court rules." Don't worry if it all seems overwhelming at first. The more time you spend with the information, the easier it will be to understand (and again, you don't have to understand the minutiae, just the broad strokes on service, response times, and such).

Not all creditor lawsuits are created equal. Four different creditor situations could exist to form the basis of the suit:

1. You are sued by the original creditor (the credit card company)

2. You are sued by a successor creditor (such as when one bank buys or merges with another bank)

3. You are sued by a debt-buyer who has purchased your account from the original creditor

4. Your account is assigned to arbitration

Arbitration is when your case does not go to trial but is heard by a neutral third-party called an arbitrator; some credit card agreements stipulate arbitration as the means for settling a debt dispute instead of litigation. Though it is important to note that the NAF (National arbitration Forum) and AAF (American Arbitration

Forum) will no longer hear or rule on consumer arbitration issues thanks to the aforementioned lawsuit filed by the Minnesota Attorney General, arbitration is now used by local courts as a form of what they call ADR (Alternative Dispute Resolution), which could also include mediation. The good news is that court-ordered ADR is *non-binding* and can therefore be challenged.

Answering the Complaint

How you respond to the Complaint depends on the creditor situation (our Lawsuit Defense Partner Program can steer you in the right direction here as well). In general, however, you will respond to the complaint by answering line-by-line the allegations brought by the Plaintiff with an admission or denial of the specifics of each allegation. For example, item #1 on the complaint might read something like this:

"(Plaintiff) is a national bank duly authorized and chartered by the state of (whatever state) to do business in this state."

While that sounds like a factual statement, how do you know it is in fact true? Your response to that portion of the complaint could be:

"Defendant has insufficient information with respect to the material allegations contained in item #1 of plaintiff's complaint and can neither admit nor deny the claims. As such defendant calls on plaintiff to prove claim."

Remember, don't make their job any easier by admitting to something they should have to prove. The more they have to prove the more likely they are to give up or mess up!

Or you might wish to admit that a claim is true. Item #2 might state:

"Defendant is a resident of (your county)."

If you are in fact a resident of that county, you could respond:

"As regards to item #2, defendant admits the material allegations contained in item #2."

Your goal is to address each count. You can do so item by item, or in some instances (which vary by state) you might simply summarize by using language such as:

"Defendant denies each of the material allegations contained in items #2, 3, 4, and 5 and calls on the plaintiff to prove those allegations and provide strict proof thereof."

Then, in most cases you will add language at the end of your answer similar to:

"Plaintiff has failed to state a claim upon which relief can be granted."

This statement challenges the legal sufficiency of the entire proceeding: there is no injury, no damage—just a claim for money.

You will file your answer to the complaint with the county clerk within 14 to 30 days, depending on the requirements in your state. Copies of your answer are mailed to the plaintiff's attorney. It is important to note that in a few states (Washington, for example) a debt collection attorney can draw up pleading papers and you have 20 days to answer the attorney, not the court. In those cases you are not served with a court summons, but with a complaint from a collection attorney. After you respond, the attorney should let you know whether they plan to file a suit or not. Just to be safe, you should call your county clerk about a week after you respond to see if the creditor lawsuit has been filed. (You can call the county clerk at any time to see if a suit has been filed against you.)

Next you will mention that you plan to initiate a process called "discovery."

Discovery

Discovery is the pre-trial phase in a lawsuit in which each party can obtain evidence from the opposing party by means of discovery devices such as requests for answers to interrogatories, requests for production of documents, and requests for admissions.

For example, a request for admission could seek to determine if the party bringing the suit is in fact the owner of the debt. In some cases the debt collector may claim they are working on behalf of the original creditor, which is not in fact true. If the debt collector cannot prove they own the debt, then they have no case.

Your goal in discovery is to require the creditor to prove that you owe the money in question, that the sum you allegedly owe is correct, and that they have a legal right to collect on the alleged debt.

Our Lawsuit Defense Partner Program can show you how to file motions, including discovery motions, in a creditor lawsuit. Once you do, there are three basic ways the suit may be dismissed based on discovery issues:

1.   **You send requests for admissions**, the creditor does not respond, your requests are deemed admitted, and you move for summary judgment and dismissal.

2.   **You file interrogatories and requests for production of documents** proving that you owe the debt, how the alleged debt was calculated, and that the plaintiff is legally entitled to collect on the account. If the plaintiff doesn't respond in a timely or appropriate manner you can ask the court to compel them to answer. If they still don't answer completely, you can move for dismissal.

3.   **You send discovery** and the creditor decides the hassle isn't worth it and *they* put in a notice for voluntary dismissal.

Other Affirmative Defenses

Remember when we talked about affirmative defenses, like disputing a debt? In most credit card debt lawsuits, creditors do not respond—either fully or at all—to a number of affirmative defenses. Their lack of response may work in your favor. Here are a few examples of affirmative defenses:

1.   **Failure to respond to billing error disputes**. If you filed a billing error dispute and the original creditor did not respond adequately, you may be able to

show that the debt is (at least partially) under dispute and therefore no judgment should be awarded.

2. **Failure of consideration**. Remember in the Debt Relief section you learned that your signature on a credit card contract is monetized and effectively funds your account? You gave the credit card company value by signing their contract. What did you get in return? A piece of plastic.

3. **Credit card agreements can be unconscionable**. The terms of most credit card agreements are incredibly one-sided and can be changed at any time by the credit card company. Sometimes they are so one-sided that a judge will decide the credit card company in effect took advantage of you.

4. **Failure to validate and subject matter jurisdiction**. Once you request verification and validation, if the information provided by the credit card company is not sufficient, they are barred under the FDCPA from pursuing collection activities. Since the FDCPA is federal, not civil, the civil court lacks subject matter jurisdiction.

5. **Assumption of risk**. The premise of this defense is that the credit card company and debt collector assumes the risk of offering credit, and assumes the risk of failing to collect on that debt.

One affirmative defense you will almost always be able to use is to claim the plaintiff's attorney has violated the FDCPA by not validating the debt (since in most cases you can argue the debt was not validated in an appropriate manner). A violation of the FDCPA is a denial of the due process rights guaranteed to you, creating a major obstacle for the debt collector to overcome.

During discovery the debt collector's attorney will almost always file a motion for summary judgment—they want the judge to decide the case without a hearing. If you have reasonable affirmative defenses, the likelihood of a summary judgment is slim; the judge will feel you deserve the right to be heard in court. If the debt collector's attorney fails to respond sufficiently to your requests for discovery, you may be able to file for your own summary judgment and have the case dismissed.

As you can tell, the litigation process is like a game—you just have to know the rules. This overview is not exhaustive by any means, but it is meant to orient you in the overall process. Again, you probably shouldn't try to deal with a debt collection lawsuit all alone. Request a free consultation from our Lawsuit Defense Partner Program at DebtClear.com.

If You Go To Trial

Despite your best efforts during the pre-trial phase, you might not be able to have the debt collection lawsuit dismissed and you might have to argue your case at trial. What should you do?

Of course the answer, again, depends on your particular situation. Make sure you discuss your particular case with an attorney or our Lawsuit Defense Partner and understand the pros and cons of proceeding to trial.

In general, here are a few major points to consider:

1. **Do you have any affirmative defenses?** Affirmative defenses give you a much stronger case and increase the likelihood that you will be able to have the case dismissed.

2. **Did they fail to comply with any discovery requests?** If so it might be because they don't have the information. If they can't prove that you owe the debt, that they are legally entitled to collect on the debt, and/or fully account for how they calculated what you owe, you have a good chance of having the lawsuit dismissed.

3. **Do you have money to settle?** I told you at the beginning of this program to save as much money as you can for settlements and/or in case you are sued. Now might be a good time to consider settling. There are no guarantees that you will win, and if you lose, you will be responsible for additional court and attorney fees. You can always wait until after you lose to offer a settlement, but as a rule you will get a better deal if you settle prior to trail.

4. **What is the worst-case scenario?** Obviously the worst-case scenario is that you lose. However, what would that mean to you in practical terms? There will be a negative hit to your credit report, but do you need good credit in the near-term? Do you own a home, and if so, does your state have a homestead exemption? Can your wages be garnished, or is your income exempt from garnishment? Do you have any other assets they can go after? What are the debt

collection laws in your state and the statute of limitations on judgments? Check out the section on Asset Protection to help answer these questions.

In many cases the lawyer will call and offer a settlement before the trial. Most lawyers are given fairly wide latitude by their clients to settle; they usually have permission to settle for half or more of the outstanding balance. Give them a chance to make an offer. Then, whatever it is, counter-offer with no more than one-third of their offer. If you owe $20,000 and they offer $10,000, counter-offer with $3,000 or so. (You can't get it if you don't ask.) Make sure you thoroughly understand the section on Negotiated Settlements (found in the Roadmap section of this book) and what needs to be contained in a settlement agreement before proceeding.

If you do decide to go to trial, my suggestion is that you get some first-hand experience. Go to court before your trial date, and just sit in the audience area and observe what happens. You'll quickly get a sense for what goes on during the average trial (it's not as scary or complicated as you might think). You might see an attorney who impresses you, or an individual who argues like crazy and gets the judge on their side. A key preparation step is learning how the system works and seeing how the key players behave.

Thoroughly review the documents you were provided during discovery. Has the creditor provided any materials? What did they provide? What is missing? What does and doesn't make sense? Review your case, documents, and strategy with our Lawsuit Defense Partner, and make sure you understand what and what *not* to do or say. Preparation is obviously key, so do your best to prepare for trial.

A final consideration is that you might want to hire an attorney rather than (or in addition to) enrolling in our Lawsuit Defense Partner Program. Some of you might feel too uncertain about the subject matter, or simply be uncomfortable arguing your case in open court. Others might have significant assets to protect and want to hire an attorney who specializes in this area. Any reputable debt attorney should give you a free consultation and recommend a course of action and fee schedule. Contact your local state bar association or go to DebtClear.com for a referral.

A Final Note

There is a fine line you must walk when presenting your case in court during a creditor lawsuit. You might be asked, point blank, whether the alleged debt is yours (or something else you feel might damage or even kill your case).

Never lie—don't perjure yourself—but it is perfectly reasonable to say that you are unsure. The creditor is the one bringing the case against you. They are alleging that you owe them money, that they are legally entitled to collect on that alleged debt, and that the amount they are alleging you owe is correct. It is up to the *creditor* to prove it, not the other way around.

It is perfectly acceptable to state that you don't know the answer to a question. Anything that you or the creditor might say that isn't backed up by actual documentation is merely hearsay.

If someone who says I owe them money were to sue me and asked me to admit that I owe them, I might respond, "I cannot make a legal determination until I see the original documents or other admissible evidence relative to this assertion."

That way you're not saying yes, you're not saying no, you are simply saying you can't answer until you are given information that helps you refresh your memory or in some way clears up a concern or question you have. Bottom line: don't make the plaintiff's case any easier by admitting anything that might help their case.

Chapter Nineteen
Judgments

Despite your best efforts, at the end of a debt collection lawsuit the judge may rule in the creditor's favor and award a judgment against you. This, of course, is the worst-case scenario, but you still have options. Make sure you read and understand the Asset Protection section (and note the warning about fraudulent conveyance).

A judgment is simply a ruling by a court of *limited* jurisdiction in regards to a creditor lawsuit. The judgment regarding your debt liability is only good in your state, not in another state. If you moved to another state a creditor could try to have the judgment domesticated to the new state, but in practical terms, this seldom happens. It's too expensive, too much trouble, and there is too much lower-hanging fruit.

A judgment is limited by time as well. Each state gives the winning party a specific amount of time to enforce the judgment. But keep in mind some states let a creditor renew the judgment; that means even if the initial term of the judgment expires, you may still have the debt hanging over your head for a much longer period of time. All you have to do to find out if a judgment against you has been renewed is to ask the court after the initial statute of limitations has expired.

How long is a judgment valid? Check out the chart below (and verify again with your court). You'll also see the interest rate

allowed on judgments and whether a judgment can be renewed
and how often.

State	Years Valid	Interest Rate	Renewable
Alabama	20	12%	No
Alaska	10	7.5%	No
Arizona	5	10%	Yes, each 5 years
Arkansas	10	10%	Yes
California	10	10%	Yes, each 10 years
Colorado	20	8%	Yes, each 20 years
Connecticut	20	10%	No
Delaware	3	9.5%	No
Florida	20	10%	Yes, at 7 years
Georgia	7	12%	No
Hawaii	10	10%	Yes
Idaho	5	10.5%	Yes
Illinois	20	9%	No
Indiana	20	10%	Yes
Iowa	10	T-bill rate	Yes, at 9 years
Kansas	5	10%	Yes
Kentucky	15	12%	No
Louisiana	10	About 6.7%	No
Maine	20	15%	Maybe
Maryland	12	15%	No
Massachusetts	20	12%	Yes
Michigan	10	About 6%	Yes
Minnesota	10	About 5%	No
Mississippi	7	Court set	No
Missouri	10	Contract rate	No
Montana	10	9%	No
Nebraska	5	Bond rate +1%	Yes, each 5 years
Nevada	6	Prime rate +2%	No
New Hampshire	20	6.5%	No
New Jersey	20	None specified	No
New Mexico	14	8.75%	No

New York	20	9%	Yes
North Carolina	10	8%	No
North Dakota	10	12%	Yes
Ohio	20	10%	Yes, each five years
Oklahoma	5	T-bill rate +4%	Yes
Oregon	10	9%	Yes
Pennsylvania	5	6%	Yes
Rhode Island	20	12%	No
South Carolina	10	14%	No
South Dakota	10	10%	Yes
Tennessee	10	10%	No
Texas	10	10%	Yes
Utah	8	Contract rate	No
Vermont	8	12%	No
Virginia	20	9%	No
Washington	10	12%	Yes
Washington, DC	20	70% of IRS tax rate	No
West Virginia	10	10%	No
Wisconsin	20	12%	No
Wyoming	5	10%	No

Once a judgment has been awarded, the creditor will try to enforce (collect) the judgment. All of this information is covered in much greater detail in the Asset Protection section, but let's review the basic things they can try to do.

1. **Take money from your bank account(s).** If you bank in the state in which judgment was awarded, the judgment creditor (the creditor who sued you and won a judgment against you) will petition the court to garnish your bank account and then ask the court to send a writ of garnishment to whatever bank they think you bank at. *Think* is the operative word here. They have to guess where you bank. They usually

just have a writ of garnishment served on the top 5 local banks in your area—and they usually get lucky. Next your funds will be frozen and they will use this as leverage to get you to enter into some type of payment plan (most people don't have enough cash in their accounts to satisfy a judgment). The lesson here is to bank online with an out-of-state bank.

2. **Garnish your wages.** While state law limits how much of your wages can be garnished, in most cases a creditor can garnish up to approximately 25% of your take home pay until the judgment is satisfied. If you quit your job and find a new one, the creditor will have to "track down" your new employment, but that is not particularly difficult. (North Carolina, South Carolina, Pennsylvania, and Texas do not allow wages to be garnished at all in order to satisfy a judgment; other states set limits on how much of your wages can be garnished.) If your state allows for garnishment, 25% of your take-home pay could be at risk. If you have multiple judgment creditors trying to garnish your wages they all have to get in line (garnishment allowances are per paycheck, not per creditor). Of course, if you quit and move to another state then garnishment will no longer be an option for the creditor. Social Security, disability benefits, Veterans payments and the like are all exempt from garnishment. Again, see the section on Asset Protection and your state's garnishment laws for more information.

3. **Put a lien on your property.** A creditor could attach a lien to your home. In almost all cases the lien will be placed on real estate and not on cars, furniture, and other assets. While they can't foreclose on your home, if you decide to sell your home, the creditor (assuming the buyer wants a clean title) will get the amount of the judgment, plus interest, before you receive any of the proceeds from the sale. The good news is that a lien expires when the judgment expires so if you plan on keeping your home, a lien has little effect and will eventually expire. Though liens can be placed on your property they generally are not; creditors want cash and cash flow, not liens against property that may not be sold for years.

The bottom line is that if a judgment creditor doesn't know where you bank, or work, and you don't own a home (or you do but don't plan on selling), the judgment is essentially worthless. Move to another state, and the judgment is essentially worthless. Self-employed and bank out of state? Also worthless. It is no wonder that the vast majority (around 80%) of judgments are uncollectable—as a group, people with creditor judgments against them usually don't have many, if any, assets to collect on anyway.

Remember that the goal of responding to a creditor lawsuit and asserting your rights is to make it too difficult and expensive for creditors to collect—to become high-hanging fruit. Most creditors are looking for a default judgment rather than to have to prove their case through lengthy and costly litigation. With so many judgments uncollectable, their profit margin dwindles quickly the harder it is to prove their case and/or enforce a judgment.

Remember, debt collection is business, so know your rights, play the game, and increase your chances for success!

Asset Protection

Chapter Twenty
Protecting Your Assets

Rich or poor, young or old, asset protection is a good idea. The U.S. is the most litigious country in the world and odds are you will be sued more than once in your lifetime. With so many things outside of our control—such as someone falling and injuring their self on your property—why not do everything you can to protect the assets for which you have worked so hard?

Asset protection can also make the difference between whether someone decides to sue you at all. One of the first things an attorney will do if they are thinking about suing you is an asset search. This helps them determine whether suing you is likely to result in a judgment they can collect on, and justifies the cost of the suit and enforcement.

As I have said before, debt collection is business, not personal.

The good news for you is that the majority of judgments are uncollectable (estimates put it at around 80%). This isn't because there is anything wrong with the judgments, but because enforcing a judgment can be very difficult for the collector.

Let's find out why, and what you can do to become high-hanging fruit!

Bank Out of State

The easiest thing for a judgment creditor (a creditor that has a judgment against you) to do is go after money in your bank account. After receiving a judgment against you, they will petition the court to garnish your bank account and then ask the court to send a writ of garnishment to whatever bank they think you bank at.

Notice, I said where they *think* you bank. Unless you told them where you bank (and if you have already read the Debt Relief section, you will know that is a big no-no) they are going to have to make some educated guesses.

First, they are probably going to try to determine where your last payments to their account came from. Creditors must have figured out by now that it makes sense to keep copies of checks just for this purpose (if not, I hope there aren't any creditors reading this!). Ask yourself, are you still banking at the same bank you were with before you went into default? Nine times out of ten, the answer will be "yes."

Most collectors are not going to have your banking information, so they take a shotgun approach. They look up the major banks in your area and have the court send a writ of garnishment to them all. Again, chances are you bank with one of them (well, do you?).

My point is that they have to find your account before they can access your funds. Your funds will actually be frozen for 30 days or so because you can ask the court for an exemption hearing in case your income, for example, is exempt from collection. Of course, no one is going to tell you this, least of all the judgment creditor. You won't know what has happened until you start bouncing checks and call your bank.

If this were to happen to you, the judgment creditor would be in a great negotiation position. They know you have to pay your bills, and the amount of money in your account is likely much less than you owe, so they agree to unfreeze your funds if you agree to some sort of payment plan.

You do not want to be in that position, especially when it is so easy to avoid.

Judgments are only good in the state where they are issued. So, if you bank out of state, any writ of garnishment from your state is unenforceable. Theoretically speaking, the judgment creditor could domesticate the judgment to the state that your out-of-state account is in, but they would have to find it first, and that would require a very large shotgun!

Furthermore, to domesticate a judgment to another state costs time and money, and unless the amount you owe is Significant (with a capital "S"), it is probably a waste of the judgment creditor's time.

Rather than driving across your state line, just hop onto your computer and set up an account online with a company like eTrade, Fidelity, or INGDirect. Don't close your local accounts, just keep the majority of your cash in the out-of-state account in case a creditor finds your local account.

Think of your local account as the possum, the decoy. Let them find it, take the little money they might find there, and then, hopefully, go away.

If you've stopped making payments and are putting that money aside to use when negotiating a settlement with creditors at a later date, it is particularly important to put those funds in an out-of-state account.

Setting up an out-of-state account is easy to do and a very effective asset protection strategy. Do it now.

Wage Garnishment

The good news is that the majority of judgment creditors do not use wage garnishment. Again, they have to find out where you work and jump through the hoops to enforce the garnishment. Also, in some states garnishing wages is actually NOT allowed. Check with your state's Attorney General's Office and/or search the Internet for "yourstate wage garnishment law."

Note: all states allow garnishment for child support, alimony, taxes, and federal student loans.

Furthermore, certain types of income are exempt from wage garnishment such as:

- Social Security
- Pensions
- Veteran's benefits
- Unemployment benefits
- Public assistance, disability, or worker's compensation benefits

Again, check your state's current laws to determine with certainty whether your income is exempt from wage garnishment.

Unfortunately, once a garnishment levy has been served on your employer they have to comply. However, it stands to reason that your creditor has to find your employer first. Since I know you didn't tell them where you worked (right?), they are going to have to try to find that information somewhere else. Do you know where they find that information 99% of the time? *On your credit report.* If you want to have that information removed from your report, you will find the necessary tools in the Credit Repair section of this book.

If you find yourself in a wage garnishment situation you still have a few choices:

1. There may be things you can do to reduce the effect of the garnishment, such as increasing 401K contributions or having more taxes withheld from your paycheck. Talk to a tax professional to learn more.

2. You can change jobs. Getting another job in-state, or even better, taking an out-of-state job would make it very unlikely the garnishment would follow you. To

really make sure, take an out-of-state job in a state that doesn't allow for garnishing wages!

3.   Become self-employed. Garnishing wages for W2 employees is easy. Garnishing wages for 1099 (independent contractors) is difficult.

The last thing to know about wage garnishment is that the maximum amount allowed by state law is in total, not per judgment creditor. Therefore, if you already have a judgment creditor taking 25% of your take-home pay, another one can't garnish your same paycheck. They will just have to get in line.

Note: I have heard of some folks getting a "friendly" judgment creditor to garnish their wages to prevent another "not-so-friendly" judgment creditor from garnishing their wages.

Liens on Property

A much less likely 3rd technique a judgment creditor will use to enforce a judgment is to put a lien on your home. I have never heard of a judgment creditor of an unsecured account going after a car or other personal property, so you probably don't need to worry about those assets.

A quick search of the public tax records will tell a judgment creditor whether you own a home or not, so why don't more judgment creditors put liens on property? Because they are largely ineffective. Here's why.

Most people live in their homes a very long time. A property lien cannot make you sell your home; it just sits there until you want to sell your home. If you want to sell, most buyers are going to want a clean title and so you will likely have to satisfy the lien to complete the sale of your home.

However, a lien is only valid for as long as the judgment is valid. Eventually, the statue of limitations on the judgment will expire and so will the lien—and if you are planning on living in your house for a while, you probably won't notice a thing.

The bottom line is that liens on property cost money and are largely ineffective. It's not that they don't happen, but they are the least employed method of judgment collection.

Note: if you live in a community property state, creditors can come after you *and* your spouse's assets, so having property in the other's name won't provide any protection.

Homestead Declaration Laws

Even though placing a lien on property is the least frequently employed method of judgment collection, there is another step you can take to protect yourself in the event a creditor *does* go after the equity in your home. After all, why not be extra careful? If you're like most Americans, your greatest asset is your home, especially if you've lived there for a number of years and have built up a lot of equity. Why not do everything you can to protect it?

All you have to do is file a Homestead Declaration with your state before a judgment is awarded, then judgment creditors cannot touch part or all of your equity, depending on the rules in your state.

Here's an example. Say you live in Massachusetts, own a home, and that home is your principal residence. Simply go to your local county office and fill out the "Declaration of Estate of Homestead" form (that's what they call it in Massachusetts). It's a simple form that asks for basic information—you won't need a lawyer or other professional to help fill it out.

If you live in Massachusetts, once the form is filed you are protected against attachment up to $500,000. In other words, if you have less than $500,000 equity in the home, it's now safe from liens by judgment creditors.

And if that's not enough reason, filing a Declaration of Estate of Homestead form can also protect the value of your home if you pass away. The residence is protected until your surviving spouse remarries or dies and until your youngest unmarried child reaches the age of 18. If the judgment expires in the meantime, your family's equity is still safe even though you're no longer around.

Keep in mind that every state is different. In Virginia, for example, the Homestead Exemption is limited to $5,000. While that pales in comparison to Massachusetts' Homestead Exemption, it is still worth the nominal filing fee.

Some states do not provide homestead rights at all, some require you to file a Homestead Declaration, and others provide homestead exemptions without requiring you to file at all. Here's a breakdown:

No Homestead Rights
Delaware
New Jersey
Pennsylvania
Rhode Island

Homestead Declaration Must Be Filed
Alabama
Louisiana
Massachusetts
Mississippi
Montana
Nebraska

Homestead Declaration *Not* Required
Alaska
Kentucky
Michigan
Missouri
Nevada
New Mexico

If your state is not listed above, filing is considered to be "elective"; you can choose to do so or not. What should you do? File the

Homestead Declaration today! (Visit the Asset Protection section at DebtClear.com for forms and filing instructions.)

It only makes sense. If you are fortunate enough to live in a state that has enacted homestead laws, why *wouldn't* you file a Homestead Declaration as soon as possible? Always do everything possible to protect your legal rights. And besides, your state requirements may change without you noticing—after all, how often do you check to see what your state legislature is up to?

To determine the specific filing rules and guidelines for your state, do a web search using the terms "homestead declaration yourstate", or call your local county office. In some cases you will be required to file the form in person or have it notarized, so make sure you ask questions to learn exactly how the process works.

And while we're talking about Homesteads, in some states you can also file what is called a Homestead Exemption (some locals use this term interchangeably with Homestead Declaration), which provides exemption from some portion of the real estate taxes you are required to pay each year.

For example, if you live in Texas and your home is worth $200,000, you may qualify for a Homestead Exemption of $15,000, meaning property tax will only be assessed against $185,000 in value. And if you're over 65, you qualify for an additional $10,000 exemption. Some counties in Georgia offer what is called a "Homestead Valuation Freeze Exemption," which is a fancy way of saying your property taxes won't go up even if the value of your home does. Again, every state is different, so check your particular state tax codes to see what applies to you. Or, simply ask at your county offices; they can fill you in.

Fraudulent Conveyance

A fraudulent conveyance is a transfer of money or property from a debtor to someone or something else when either: 1) the debtor intends to deliberately hide their assets from creditors, and/or 2) the debtor received less than a reasonably equivalent value in exchange for the transfer of property (such as selling your house to your brother for $1 to avoid a lien).

Each state has laws on the books that determine the timeframe during which a creditor can make a fraudulent conveyance claim. To be clear, fraudulent conveyance isn't a prohibition on asset protection, it just limits the *timeframe* between when you protected an asset and when a judgment was awarded. Usually the timeframe is 2 years, but you should check with a reputable source in your state to confirm the timeframe.

If a creditor alleges fraudulent conveyance, they would have to sue you in civil court and prove that you had intentionally moved money or property to avoid paying them. For reasons that are likely obvious to you by now, this hardly ever happens unless a bankruptcy court is involved.

For any attorneys that might be reading this, I am not suggesting that anyone commit fraudulent conveyance; readers should check the laws in their state and abide by them. However, people open up new bank accounts, quit their jobs, move or choose not to sell their homes every day. It is highly unlikely that a judgment creditor is going to pursue a fraudulent conveyance claim, let alone be successful in proving one.

Enough said.

LLCs, Corporations, and Trusts

In the early days of asset protection, everyone was touting the protections of putting everything you owed into a business entity such as an LLC or Corporation. Because of the deliberate abuse of using companies as asset protection vehicles, there are now many laws on the books that make them ineffective as a way to shield your assets from creditors.

You will find a lot of conflicting information on the Internet about this, so it is best to consult with a licensed professional in your state. My take is that it is probably more trouble than it is worth and certainly screams fraudulent conveyance if done within the state-defined timeframe.

Trusts, on the other hand, can and do provide excellent asset protection. However, they are very expensive to set up and maintain and, unless you have significant assets to protect, this is going to be a waste of your time and money. If you think a trust might be a good way to protect your assets, make sure you consult with a licensed professional and shop around.

Keep Separate Accounts

If you're married and have a joint bank account, that account can be levied by creditors seeking to satisfy a judgment. If you are the sole person responsible for the debt—meaning the credit card account was in your name only—then they can only go after accounts with your name on them. If you live in a community property state (Arizona, California, Idaho, Louisiana, Nevada, New Mexico, Texas, Washington, and Wisconsin), a judgment creditor can go after you and your spouse's accounts and income. All the more reason to keep accounts separate and harder to find.

Keep a Little Cash on Hand

If the worst does happen and a judgment is entered against you, some or all of your accounts might quickly be attached or even frozen. If that occurs, you'll still need money, so keep a cash emergency fund handy. That way you can take care of day-to-day expenses even if you don't have access to most of your assets, even for a short period of time.

Roadmap

Chapter Twenty-One
Overview of the Process

First things first: if you haven't read the sections on Debt Relief, Credit Repair, Lawsuits, and Asset Protection, stop.

Go back. Read them all. Take the time to understand the laws, the guidelines, and every single bit of the background information. Knowledge is power, and the only way to be at full debt relief power is to put all the knowledge at your disposal to work. The Roadmap is an *overview* of the process. It will help you understand where you are on the road to debt freedom and the signposts, forks, and pitfalls that lie ahead. It does not contain all the information you need to make informed decisions about what to do at each stage of the process.

The other sections of this book are intended to educate you about the players, the playing field, and the rules of the game so you can make the best decisions for you given your unique situation. You can't make great decisions without the right information.

So if you haven't already, go back and read those sections. *Now.* Once you do, you'll be ready to take all the knowledge you have gained to accelerate down the road to financial freedom.

Again, this is a fairly high level overview; refer back to the appropriate section any time you have questions or are in any way unsure about how to proceed. Also, please make sure you utilize the other resources available to you online at DebtClear.com—the

Blog, Forum, FAQ, Resource Library, and referrals to trusted service providers.

Now, on to the Roadmap!

Let's walk through the debt relief process from start to finish and identify the steps you should take along the way:

1. You take steps to protect your assets from creditors and from others.

2. You stop—for whatever reason—making payments on a credit card.

3. You start saving as much money as you can for settlements, if needed.

4. The credit card company calls and sends letters. You never admit the debt is yours. In fact, you never admit anything and you give the credit card company no information whatsoever.

5. You decide to dispute a billing error on an item or items on a credit card bill in order to create an affirmative defense, or

6. You decide not to dispute a billing error on a credit card bill, either because there is nothing to dispute or you don't want to put the credit card company on notice that you're playing offense.

7. After 180 days of non-payment, the original creditor writes off the debt and sells or assigns the debt to a debt collector.

8. The debt collector sends a dunning letter giving you 30 days to dispute the debt. You should always respond with a dispute and verification and validation request, even if is has been more than 30 days.

9. You assert your rights under the FDCPA and keep detailed records of all calls and correspondence—your goal is to collect violations under the FDCPA that you can use as an affirmative defense if you are sued. You can also use the threat of a federal lawsuit, or an actual lawsuit, to force the creditor to settle even before a lawsuit is filed.

10. You begin credit repair.

11. You decide at any point whether you would like to use the funds you have saved to settle the debt. (Note that in some cases, settlements can void your limited money-back guarantee with us).

12. If the creditor files a suit and you receive a summons, you immediately enroll in our Lawsuit Defense Partner Program or hire an attorney.

13. You respond to the creditor's summons in a timely and appropriate manner; **you never stick your head in the sand and fail to respond** because, if you do, you automatically lose.

14. You determine the worst-case scenario if a judgment is won against you. (Losing the suit may not have much of an impact, depending on your situation.)

15. You review discovery with our Lawsuit Defense Partner or your attorney and devise a strategy. Prepare, prepare, prepare!

16. You decide whether you want to settle or take your chances in court.

17. You continue repairing any damage to your credit, both during the debt relief process and after. You decide whether you want to settle or take your chances in court.

18. Once the statute of limitations has been reached on your debt throw yourself a party!

Chapter Twenty-Two
The 5 Mile Markers

Mile Marker 1: Original Creditors

Step One: Stop Making Payments

To be clear (again), I am not telling you not to pay your creditors. However, some of you may be struggling to make your minimum payments, or know that you won't be able to service your debt any longer for reasons outside your control. The reality is this: unless you stop making your payments, you will not experience any debt relief, or start the statute of limitations clock on your debt.

Action Steps:

1. Stop making payments for whatever reason.

2. Mark your calendar for 180 days from the date of your last payment; that is when the original creditor will usually charge off your account.

Once you stop making payments, you'll soon find yourself at Mile Marker 2 on the Roadmap.

Mile Marker 2: Pre Charge-Off

Step One: Determine Your Debt Relief Start Date

The statute of limitations clock starts ticking beginning on the day of your last payment, or the date your account is charged off. Check with your state's Attorney General's Office on the exact method for calculating your statute of limitations, then go to your calendar and put a big red X on that date. After this date, your debt is considered a time-barred debt and creditors can no longer sue you to collect, but the clock doesn't start ticking until you stop making payments.

Regardless of your state's statute of limitations, we see the majority of lawsuits happening in the first couple years (though you can technically be sued up until the statue of limitations expires).

Action Steps:

1. Determine when you made your last payment to each of your accounts.

2. Mark your calendar for 180 days from the due date of your last payment(s); that is when the original creditor will charge off your account.

3. Check the statute of limitations in your state and how to calculate it.

4. Mark your calendar on the date your debt(s) will become time-barred.

5. Do not make any more payments unless you choose to settle the account; doing so will reset the statute of limitations clock.

Step Two: Start Saving as Much Money as You Can

Save as much money as you can. You'll set aside these funds for two main purposes. One, you can use that money for settlements in case you are sued and are not able to have the case dismissed (or you reach an acceptable settlement prior to being sued). Two, since the likelihood of being sued is relatively low, once the statute of limitations runs out on your debt you can use your savings to invest in your financial future.

So no matter what, don't spend your excess cash—save it!

Let's take a quick step back. I have three reasons for helping you get out of debt:

1. I want to help you get as much debt relief as possible.

2. We don't like repeat customers! I want to educate you about the cycle of debt and interest that got you into this situation in the first place, and teach you better habits.

3. I want you to use the power of compound interest in your favor to help you build financial security.

So stop making payments and start saving today, preferably in an interest-bearing account.

Action Steps:

1. Start saving as much money as you can.

2. Keep those savings in a bank account out-of-state.

3. Don't commingle funds from protected income like pensions and Social Security.

Step Three: Protect Your Assets

Remember when I mentioned how difficult it is for a creditor to enforce a judgment? There are things you can and should do *right now* to make it even *more* difficult.

Take a quick drive to the next state, or better yet open a savings or brokerage account online (just make sure there are no in-state offices). Remember, a judgment is limited in jurisdiction—it is only good for the state in which it was awarded. Maintain your current local accounts, but keep most of your actual money out of state.

Next, see if your state allows for a Homestead Declaration and if you are required to file a declaration (some states offer defacto protection). In practical terms, this means a certain dollar value of your home is protected from your creditors.

Lastly, to garnish wages a judgment creditor needs to know where you work. Don't make this any easier by displaying this information on your credit report.

Action Steps:

1. Create an out-of-state savings account.

2. Make sure you and your spouse have separate accounts, regardless of whether you live in a community property state.

3. Check to see if your state allows for a Homestead Declaration; if it does, file the form immediately.

4. While you're at it, see if your state allows a Homestead Exemption that reduces the amount of real estate property tax you are required to pay.

5. If you are a W2 employee, consider becoming self-employed and removing any employment information from your credit report.

Step Four: Give Thought to Settling with the Original Creditor

If your account(s) are still with the original creditor, you may choose to settle the account after 4-5 months of non-payment, just before the original creditor charges-off your account. In many cases, the original creditor will initiate a settlement offer—you won't even have to raise the subject yourself.

Either way, for most people the biggest problem with settling is that you will need enough cash to make a lump sum payment in order to settle. Make sure you thoroughly review the pros and cons of settlement in the Settlement section below so you make an informed decision. Also note that settling at this stage in the game will void the guarantee that came with this book.

In the end, do what is right for you, but don't wait until the original creditor calls to give the issue some thought. Start thinking about it today.

Mile Marker 3: Debt Collectors

After six months of non-payment, the original creditor will likely write off your account as bad debt and debt collectors will start contacting you. If you don't understand the difference between original creditors and debt collectors, then go back and read the Debt Relief section.

Step One: Respond to Dunning Letters

Federal law requires that you be sent a dunning letter five days after the debt collector makes initial contact. Also remember that the "dunning letter" can be delivered verbally, as long as the debt collector provides the required information.

How should you respond? See the Appendix or Resource Library at DebtClear.com for a sample response to a dunning letter.

Just make sure you never volunteer any information; simply assert your right to have the debt verified. Never acknowledge the debt or your responsibility for the debt.

Always send your request for verification and validation by certified mail, return receipt requested. Keep a copy in your correspondence log.

You'll probably receive a response—but sometimes you won't. If the debt collector can't verify a debt, or simply doesn't want to take the time and incur the expense necessary to provide verification of the debt, they may drop the account or, more likely, sell the debt to another debt collector. Even those that do respond may not respond in an appropriate manner.

Action Steps:

1. Respond in writing to dunning letters (or to "dunning letter" calls) within 30 days.

2.   Use the provided templates for guidance on writing your own letters.

3.   Send your request by certified mail, return receipt requested.

4.   Keep records of all correspondence.

Step Two: Document All Communications and FDCPA Violations

Debt collectors will try to scare, intimidate, and bully you. They'll ask questions. They'll play good cop/bad cop. No matter the approach, their goal is to confirm they've reached the right person, get you to acknowledge that you owe the debt, and then work hard to get a payment, no matter how small.

Action Steps (when the debt collector calls):

1.   Ask who is calling.

2.   Record the call and give proper notice if you are in an all-party state.

3.   Go "violation fishing" or state you no longer wish to be contacted via phone. Follow up with a Do-Not-Call letter, sent certified mail with return receipt requested.

4.   Never, never, never acknowledge the debt or provide any additional information such as your address, your place of employment, etc.

5.   Don't give in to fear, guilt, or intimidation.

Then:

1. Document the call in your call log.

2. Listen carefully for FDCPA violations. We've covered these before, but stay alert for the most common violations:

   - Calls before 8 a.m. and after 9 p.m.
   - Failure to identify themselves completely when they initiate a conversation
   - Failure to send a dunning letter within five days of making initial contact
   - Continuing collection efforts or reporting negatives to the credit bureau before they have complied with your verification validation request
   - Failure to comply with your Do-Not-Call request
   - Threats, harassment, abuse, or use of profanity
   - Calling multiple times per day
   - Making false or misleading statements

Key Note: Keep in mind that how you respond to threats or harassment is important. In a way, violations of the FDCPA are like personal injury cases: emotional distress is a factor in determining damages. If you feel threatened, you often have been threatened. If you feel intimidated, by law you may actually have been intimidated, even if the debt collector did not intend to do so. The key is how you *felt*.

For example, it's possible a debt collector could stress you out so much you can't sleep or even have an anxiety attack. If that happens, *write it down*. By keeping logs and phone recordings, it's a lot easier to prove harassment because you have the documentation to back it up.

Step Three: Sue or Threaten to Sue if Your Rights Are Violated

If your rights are violated you can threaten to sue, or actually sue. The more numerous and egregious the violations, the better leverage you have against a debt collector. Consult the guidelines and charts in the Know Your Federal Rights section on Debt Relief.

Action Steps:

1. Match your documentation against the violations list.

2. If you find any violations, consult with an attorney (visit DebtClear.com for a free consultation).

3. Use the threat of a lawsuit to make them zero out the debt and update your credit report to "paid as agreed" or remove the record altogether. You may need to actually file a suit to get the leverage you need.

Step Four: Begin Credit Repair

Credit repair is a process, not an event. Once your account has been charged-off and assigned or sold to a debt collector you can begin the process of credit repair.

Remember, credit repair is more than just removing negative entries from your credit reports. Keeping older accounts in good standing open, having a good mix of credit, keeping your balances low, rebuilding credit with secured cards, etc. all work towards increasing your overall score.

Of course, removing negatives from your report can have a dramatic impact on your score, so make sure you read and understand the dispute process described in the Credit Repair section of this book and start ASAP.

Action Steps:

1. Get a current copy of your credit report from all three bureaus.

2. Start disputing negative entries.

3. Implement other credit building strategies.

Mile Marker 4: You Are Served with a Lawsuit

As you know, lawsuits are fairly rare where unsecured debt is concerned, but they can and do happen. What should you do? Just like with dunning letters, your first step is to *respond*!

Step One: Respond to Lawsuits

The Lawsuit section offers advice and guidance for dealing with a summons and responding to a lawsuit.

Action Steps:

1. Enroll in our Lawsuit Defense Partner Program or hire an attorney.

2. Answer the complaint within the specified time frame—never give up your rights!

3. Provide the information requested, but do not volunteer any additional information and never admit to anything the creditor should have to prove.

4. Request discovery and use other affirmative defenses.

5. Move to dismiss if the creditor fails to respond in a timely or appropriate manner.

Just like with a dunning letter, don't stick your head in the sand. You must respond to the lawsuit or a default judgment *will* be entered against you.

Step Two: Consider Settling the Lawsuit

If you are sued and despite your best efforts you can't have the case dismissed, consider settling using the money you started saving at Mile Marker 2.

A judgment is a hit to your credit score, and just before trial you are in a fairly good negotiating position (the creditor doesn't want to go to trial any more than you do). As always, this decision is up to you. Make sure you understand the pros and cons of settlement before you decide.

Action Steps:

1. Consult with our Lawsuit Defense Partner, or an attorney in your area.

2. Review the relevant sections in the Lawsuit section above and the Settlement section below.

3. Get everything in writing *first* and make sure your credit report is updated to "paid as agreed" or the entry is removed altogether.

Mile Marker 5: You are NOT Served with a Lawsuit

You are almost at the end of the road! If you don't settle with a creditor and aren't taken to court, this is the stage at which most of your accounts should end up.

Once the statute of limitations has expired on your debt (remember this varies by state), the debt is essentially uncollectible. If you receive a lawsuit after the statute of limitations has expired, you only need to show the court a copy of your credit report (showing the date you stopped making payments) and your state's statute of limitations.

Technically, a debt collector can still try to collect on a time-barred debt, but they can't sue you over it. Since you can (if you haven't already) send debt collectors a Do-Not-Call letter, the only thing they can legally do with time-barred debts is send you letters.

In practice, if you are going to be sued by a creditor it is usually in the first 12-18 months, and the collection attempts usually die off well before the statute of limitations is reached.

Action Steps:

1. Keep track of the date when the statute of limitations expires on your debt(s).

2. Once that date arrives, CELEBRATE! Congratulate yourself for the patience and fortitude it took you to get there.

3. Take the money in your settlement fund (if you haven't already) and pay down secured debts such as your car or mortgage, or invest it.

4. Continue to repair your credit. Just because the statute of limitations has expired on your debt doesn't mean that it disappears from your credit report. Charge-offs and collection accounts can still report on your credit report for up to 7 years.

Chapter Twenty-Three
Debt Settlement Tutorial

We've discussed settlement as an option at several points in the program. In each case I have been, frankly, less than positive when discussing the topic of settlement unless you are involved in a lawsuit. But it is always an option, so let's look more closely at the pros and cons of debt settlement.

First, the basics: the concept of debt settlement is simple. In exchange for an agreed-upon amount of money, the creditor "forgives" the rest of the debt and reports it to the credit bureaus as settled. Say you owe a creditor $10,000. The creditor offers to settle the debt for $7,000. If you pay the $7,000, the creditor agrees that the debt has been satisfied and you don't owe any more money.

Why could settling work in your favor? An obvious benefit of settlement is that you pay back only a percentage of what you originally owed. Plus, all collection activities stop, and you can usually have your credit report updated and the effect of a negative entry reduced or eliminated. The downsides of settlement are: the amount you will have to pay in settlement (that you otherwise might have kept); the potential hit to your credit score (not all creditors can or will agree to update your credit report); and last, but in no way least, the potential tax liability on the amount forgiven. Tax liability is a critical issue. In the example above, the $3,000 that was "forgiven" may be reported by the creditor to the IRS as 1099 income (less than 20% of the time), and you will have to pay taxes on that "income".

Settling should be considered a last resort in terms of this program, and doing so also voids your money-back guarantee unless used as a last resort. The reason settlement should be considered a last resort is simple: if you voluntarily settle your account(s) you are extremely likely—in fact, you're almost guaranteed—to pay back a larger percentage of what you owe. Why? If you settle, you pay some of the debt. If you don't settle the odds are that the debt will be eliminated due to the statute of limitations expiring and you will pay *nothing*. Last time I checked, *something* is always more than *nothing*.

Whether you decide to settle an account is ultimately up to you and is a decision you should never take lightly. The debt collectors and attorneys with whom you will be negotiating are professional negotiators. Their job is to talk you into agreeing to the best settlement for *them*, which, of course, will be a worse settlement for *you*. Keep in mind that they negotiate with people all day, every day; if you think used car salespeople are tough, wait until you deal with debt collectors and attorneys. If you want to hire a negotiator to work for you, just visit DebtClear.com for a referral to an accredited negotiation professional.

Finally, settlement is only an option if you have fallen behind on your payments. Think about it: why would a creditor accept less than full payment when they are being paid in full each month? Sure, you might be trying to do the responsible thing by working out a settlement *before* you go into default, but no creditor will work with you while you are still current. That just won't happen. Remember, debt collection is a business; no creditor will consider working with you or making a deal unless they are actually losing money. If you are making your payments, they are *making* money.

So let's look at the basics of settlement, just in case it does become an option you want to explore. We'll look at your options during each phase of the debt relief process, starting with original creditors.

Settling with Original Creditors

First, let's reinforce this point: if you are current on your payments, no original creditor will consider settling for less than the full amount of your balance. They don't care if you're struggling financially, they don't care if you're trying to do the "right thing", because they're making money.

So if you stop making payments, for the first few months you'll get threatening phone calls and increasingly unfriendly letters. Don't worry too much about it. Almost every original creditor threatens to sue; a much lower percentage will actually go through with filing a lawsuit. (And if they do file, you can still attempt to settle before the case goes to trial.)

That's why the first time you should considering settling with the original creditor is right before the account is charged off, at around the 4th or 5th month of non-payment. At that point, time is working against the original creditor since they usually write off the debt after six months of non-payment.

Keep in mind that an original creditor who writes off a debt doesn't take a total loss on the account. As part of the process of writing off the account, the original creditor will in most cases sell the account to a debt collector for some percentage of the amount of debt (usually between 10 to 15% of what you owe). That money goes in the credit card company's pocket. Then the credit card company is likely to have insurance on its accounts, let's call that maybe 5 to 10%. The remainder of the "loss" can be taken as a tax deduction—if the company is in the 30% bracket, that's another 20% or so. So instead of losing 100% of the amount you owe, the credit card company is recovering anywhere between 30 to 50% of your account automatically.

Obviously your settlement must be equal to or greater than what they will get by writing off your debt, otherwise, why would they settle?

Of course you will have no idea what money the credit card company stands to recover, so you'll have to negotiate. If you want to settle, start low. For instance, you could say:

"I have four credit cards and I only have enough money to settle with one or two of you. Will you take 20% of the balance as payment in-full?"

Then see if they take it. The odds are slim, but like most things, you never know unless you ask. Then raise the amount until you reach the maximum for which you would want to settle the account.

If the credit card company does offer a settlement you can afford—and you feel comfortable making—ask for a few other provisions before you finalize the agreement:

1.   Require a signed contract from the creditor stating the terms of the settlement, the amount, and that the debt will be considered satisfied and no further collection activities are allowed.

2. Include a "paid as agreed" provision. Otherwise, the creditor is likely to report your account as "settled for less than full amount" which is much more damaging to your credit score.

3. Ask that they remove any late payments from your credit report, as well. Many won't do this, but it doesn't hurt to ask.

Refer to the Appendix for an example of a settlement letter.

If you do decide to settle with an original creditor, keep in mind:

1. You might receive a 1099 showing the difference between the account balance and the settlement amount as income. If so, you will be required to pay personal income tax on that amount. The better the settlement, the more taxes you might have to pay.

2. Settling with an original creditor voids your guarantee with our program.

Important Note: Never agree to make a payment, even a small, partial payment. Once you make that payment, you immediately reset the clock and the credit card company will not write off the debt for another six months. Once you stop making payments, don't make any more payments unless you plan to exit the debt relief process and go back to making monthly payments.

Settling with Debt Collectors

Once six months has passed from the date of your first missed payment, the original creditor will likely write off the debt (that is, as long as you didn't do something silly like make a partial payment).

When a debt is written off, it is either assigned or sold. If a debt is sold, the original creditor no longer has an interest in that debt; the debt collector who purchased the debt now owns it. If the debt is assigned, the original creditor has contracted with a debt collector or collections attorney to try to collect the debt on the original creditor's behalf. In that case, they still have a "say" in the account, since they still own it.

Either way, you will still be contacted by a debt collector:

- If the debt was assigned, the original creditor is still the owner of the debt. In this case, you probably will not be able to negotiate a great deal, but you might do better than you would if you negotiated at month five or six before the account was written off. Why? The older the debt becomes the less chance there is of recovering *any* money at all. They know it and now you know it. Start at 10% of the amount of the debt, and work your way up from there.

- If the debt was sold, the debt collector has purchased the debt for 10 to 15 cents on the dollar—the debt collector has more to gain and a lot less to lose. If you agree to pay 50% of the balance as a settlement, they could make a 500% profit on their investment … not bad.

The key is to determine whether the debt was assigned or sold. When you respond to the dunning letter asking for verification and validation is the time to find this out.

No matter what, never admit responsibility for the debt. If you don't understand why, you should go back and read the Debt Relief section of this book. Always talk about settling in theoretical terms. For example, you could say, "I do not know whether this debt is mine or not. But I might decide to settle on this alleged debt just to make the whole issue go away; I can offer 10% of what you claim I owe."

And never make a partial payment. Making a partial payment is an admission of responsibility, resets the statute of limitations on the debt, and creates a contract where none existed before.

Ask for a few provisions before you finalize the agreement:

1. Require a signed contract from the debt collector (or original creditor if the debt was assigned) stating the terms of the settlement, the amount, and that the account will be satisfied and no further collection activities are allowed.

2. Include a "paid as agreed" provision. If the debt was assigned, the original creditor still owns the debt and can report the fact that the account was "paid as agreed" to the credit bureaus. If the assignee has put a negative entry on your credit report, ask them to remove the tradeline entirely. If the debt was sold, the debt collector should be able to update or remove their own negative entry, but probably can't

make the original creditor do anything to update your credit report. It doesn't hurt to ask, though.

Again, refer to the Appendix for an example of a settlement letter.

Updating Your Credit Report

If you agree to a settlement, your ultimate goal is to have the entry removed from your credit report entirely. If that is not possible, your secondary goal is to have the entry updated to "paid as agreed."

- If the account has been sold, the third-party debt collector might not be able to update the original creditor record, but it never hurts to ask.

- If the account has been assigned, both the original creditor and debt collector entries should be updated.

Either way, updating your credit report should be a non-negotiable condition of settlement. Be willing to walk away if they don't give you this concession, and negotiate this only *after* you have decided upon a settlement amount. Don't let them try to get you to pay more for updating your credit report, it doesn't cost them anything to do this.

Lawsuits and Settlement

As a negotiating tactic, many (if not all) original creditors and debt collectors will threaten to sue you. Few are in fact serious. For most, this is simply a ploy to soften you up. It is the debt collector's version of the good cop/bad cop routine.

The bad cop says, "If you don't make immediate payment, we may have no choice but to exercise our right to take legal action." That sounds scary. The good cop can then step in and say, "Look, we don't want to take you to court. That's the last thing we want to do to a nice person like you, but we will if we're forced to. So here's what I can offer …".

Always keep in mind that threats of lawsuits are fairly common; actual lawsuits are much less common. But it could happen, so what should you do if you do get sued?

If you have read the section on Lawsuits you know I am going to tell you to FIGHT IT!

Why? A better answer is, "Why not?" You have nothing to lose. Chances are you can get the suit dismissed with the help of our Lawsuit Defense Partner Program.

Even if you aren't successful in getting the suit dismissed after discovery, and it looks like you might have to go to trial, then consider settling (don't worry, your limited money-back guarantee with DebtClear will still be in effect).

Keep in mind that lawyers don't want to go to trial any more than you do. Lawyers would much rather settle; their business is a numbers game, too. Preparing for a trial, attending the trial: it all takes time, and time is money. And a judgment is a worthless piece of paper unless you can enforce it. A settlement means money in the bank for the creditor, and cash is always king.

Let the attorney make the first offer, and then counter-offer accordingly (counter with 1/3 of their offer). As with other settlements, make sure you get the agreement in writing, and make sure the agreement includes provisions stating that the creditor or debt collector will not engage in further debt collection activities and will update your credit report.

The goal with pre-trial negotiations is to let the attorney know that, even if they get a judgment, it will be next to impossible to enforce. Perhaps you don't bank in state. Perhaps your income is exempt from garnishment. Perhaps you don't own a home or even if you do, don't plan on ever selling it. If you have read the sections on Asset Protection and Lawsuits, you should have a pretty good idea of how to make an attorney believe that *any* money you pay them in settlement is going to be more than they will get with a judgment.

Also keep in mind that you can still settle even *after* a judgment is awarded against you. Maybe you offer a little more, but your situation as the judgment debtor hasn't changed—they are still going to have a very tough time collecting anything from you, especially if you have followed my advice in the Asset Protection section. So feel free to negotiate at this point too, but make sure one of your conditions is that the creditor agrees to petition the court to vacate the judgment.

"Vacating" the judgment is like "voiding" the judgment—in effect, the plaintiff (the creditor) agrees to give up its rights under the judgment. It's like the case never went to court at all.

Why should you care? Because judgments show up on your credit reports as negative entries. Once the judgment has been vacated by the court, you can dispute the judgment entry on your credit report and it should be removed. Alternatively, just send copies of the order to vacate the judgment directly to the bureaus and ask them to remove the entries.

Form 982

If you settle a debt and receive a 1099 form, you'll owe tax on the amount of money you were not required to pay to settle the debt. For example, if you owed $15,000 and settled for $5,000, you will owe income tax on the $10,000 difference if the debt collector files a 1099 form.

But you may be able to reduce your tax burden. Under certain circumstances, filing IRS Form 982, **Reduction of Tax Attributes Due to Discharge of Indebtedness,** could allow you to reduce or exclude the amount by which you benefit from the discharge of indebtedness that is included in your gross income.

In other words, under certain circumstances you may not have to pay tax on the difference. The form is, well, complicated. My best advice is to consult a tax specialist. That might cost you a little money, but it could also save you a lot of money in taxes.

To Review

1. Never admit to the debt. I can't stress that enough; that's why I keep saying it.

2. Stay calm. Original creditors and debt collectors can certainly get abusive, but they have no real power over you. If you can't stand it, hang up. That's your

right. (But if they do get abusive, document what happened during the call!)

3. Negotiate at the end of the month. Debt collectors and settlement attorneys are often like salespeople with quotas to meet. If they need the "numbers" to make their month, they may be more willing to negotiate.

4. Offer a lump sum to settle. Offering to enter a payment plan is fine, but the debt collector would greatly prefer a lump sum payment. Debt collectors want the money *now*. "Later" may never come.

5. Realize that the "supervisor" you get transferred to is probably the person in the next cubicle. That's just a sales tactic; don't buy it.

6. Never give out bank information, agree to automatic deductions, or make a payment by wire transfer or "check by phone." Once you give out personal information you can never, ever get it back.

7. Get a copy of the agreement in writing. Never make any payments until you have the agreement in writing, and are positive you understand and accept the terms of the agreement.

Think long and hard if you are offered a settlement. Think about your willingness to accept the risk of a lawsuit. Think about the likelihood of even lower settlement offers down the road. Think about the effect a settlement will likely have on your taxes.

Only you can decide what's right for you, so make the best choice for your situation. And, if you don't reach an agreement you are comfortable with—or one you can afford—keep playing the debt relief game by your rules. After all, now you have the playbook.

Chapter Twenty-Four
In Closing

This program contains knowledge and insights gained after almost a decade in the debt relief and credit repair industry. My hope is that the information has provided you with the tools and information necessary to make the best decisions for you, your family and your financial future.

But the information contained here isn't static. Laws change, new strategies emerge, and old strategies fall away. My hope is that you will take an active part in the community at DebtClear.com. Join the forum, ask questions, share what works and what doesn't, and suggest ways for us to improve the website. You are part of a community now and we are here to help one another.

DebtClear has also partnered with some of the best service providers in the industry. If we recommend a product or service at DebtClear.com, you can be sure they have been thoroughly vetted and represent the best practices in their respective industries.

In closing, I would like to welcome you to the end of the road and congratulate you on your diligence in transforming yourself from low-hanging fruit into high-hanging fruit. Not only did you save yourself a lot of money, but isn't the view great from up here?

Best wishes,

Michael Croix

Appendix

Letter Templates

Letter to Request Your Credit File

Your Full Name
Your Address
Your City, State Zip

Date

Credit Bureau Name
Credit Bureau Address
Credit Bureau City, State Zip

To Whom It May Concern:

Please accept this letter as a formal request for a copy of my credit report. **[Insert one of the following:**

- **I was denied credit by *Creditor's Name* and have enclosed a copy of the correspondence from them**
- **Per the FACTA, I am entitled to one free copy per year**
- **I am unemployed and searching for a job**
- **I have enclosed the required fee]**

My verification information is:

> Name: **[insert your name]**
> Social Security Number: **[insert your SSN]**
> Date of Birth: **[insert your DOB]**
> Current Address: **[insert your current address]**
> Previous Address: **[insert your previous address]**

I have also enclosed a copy of my state issued ID and a utility statement with my name and current address.

Sincerely,

[sign your name here]

Your Name

Letter to Request Credit Bureau Investigate a Dispute

Your Full Name
Your Address
Your City, State Zip

Date

Credit Bureau Name
Credit Bureau Address
Credit Bureau City, State Zip

To Whom It May Concern:

This letter is a formal request to correct inaccurate information contained in my credit file. The item(s) listed below **[select one: is/are] [select and** *insert appropriate word(s):* **inaccurate, incorrect, incomplete, erroneous, or outdated]**. I have enclosed a copy of the credit report your organization provided to me on **[insert date of report here]** and have circled in red the item(s) in question.

Line Item: **[insert name of creditor, account number, or line item number]**

Requested Correction: **[Describe exactly what you want. If you want an item deleted, say so and explain why. If you want an item corrected or updated, provide the correct information such as names, dates, amounts, and so forth and any evidence to support your claim]**

In accordance with 15 U.S.C. §1681i(a)(5)(A)(i), I request that you investigate my claim and, if after your investigation, you find my claim to be valid and accurate, I request that you immediately **[select one: delete, update, correct]** the item.

Furthermore, pursuant to 15 U.S.C. §1681i(b), I request that you supply a corrected copy of my credit report to me and all creditors who have received a copy within the last 6 months, or the last 2 years for employment purposes. Additionally, please provide me with the name, address, and telephone number of each credit grantor or other subscriber to whom you provided a copy of my credit report within the past six months.

If your investigation shows the information to be accurate, I request that you forward to me a description of the procedure used to determine the accuracy and completeness of the item(s) in question, including the business name and contact information of any furnisher within 15 days of the completion of your re-investigation as required by 15 U.S.C. §1681i(a)(6)(B)(iii).

You are bound by Federal Law to comply with the above requests within the time periods specified. Failure to do so will result in a complaint being filed with the Federal Trade Commission, your state's Attorney General, and a lawsuit filed against your company.

I have also enclosed a copy my state issued ID and a utility statement with my name and current address.

Sincerely,

[sign your name here]

Your Name
SSN and DOB

Credit Bureau Failure to Respond Within 37 Days

Your Full Name
Your Address
Your City, State, Zip

Date

Credit Bureau Name
Credit Bureau Address
Credit Bureau City, State Zip

To Whom It May Concern:

On **[insert date]** you received the attached letter, which I sent you certified mail with return receipt. Since you have failed to respond within the required 37 days as stipulated under section 15 U.S.C. §1681i(a)(1)(A) & (3)(B) of the FCRA, you must immediately delete the accounts referenced below from my credit report:

[list account(s) here]

As per my original request, please provide me with a complete and detailed copy of my credit showing the deletion of the above items.

THIS IS NOT A REQUEST FOR A REINVESTIGATION. YOUR FAILURE TO RESPOND TO MY INITIAL DISPUTE IN THE TIMEFRAME ALLOTTED BY THE FCRA MEANS THAT YOU MUST DELETE THESE ITEMS FROM MY CREDIT REPORT PURSUANT TO 15 U.S.C. §1681i(a)(1)(A).

IF I DON'T RECEIVE AN UPDATED COPY OF MY REPORT SHOWING THE ABOVE ITEMS DELETED WITHIN 30 DAYS OF RECEIPT OF THIS LETTER, I WILL FILE A COMPLAINT WITH THE FEDERAL TRADE COMMISSION AND YOUR STATE'S ATTORNEY GENERAL, AND FILE SUIT AGAINST YOUR COMPANY FOR DAMAGES IN FEDERAL DISTRICT COURT.

Sincerely,

[sign your name here]

Your Name
SSN and DOB

Letter of Complaint to the FTC (for Failure to Investigate)

Your Name
Your Address
Your City, State Zip

Date

Federal Trade Commission
Consumer Response Center
600 Pennsylvania Avenue, NW
Washington, DC 20580

Re: Complaint

To Whom It May Concern:

On **[insert date received]**, **[insert name of credit bureau]** received the attached dispute letter. **[insert name of credit bureau]** failed to respond to my reinvestigation request within the timeframe required by 15 U.S.C. §1681i(a)(1)(A) & (3)(B).

On **[insert date received]**, **[insert name of credit bureau]** received a second letter (also attached) notifying them of their failure to respond and demanding that the disputed items be removed pursuant to 15 U.S.C. §1681i(a)(1)(A). After another 30 days, they are still in non-compliance.

This non-compliance is causing me serious personal and financial hardship. Therefore, I am requesting that your agency assist me in this matter. I can be reached at the above address or **[insert phone numbers where you can easily be reached]**.

Thank you in advance for any help you can provide me in resolving this issue.

Sincerely,

[sign your name here]

Your Name

cc: Credit Bureau **[Send a copy to the bureau so they know of the complaint and can take action.]**

Letter to Request a Creditor Remove an Error

Your Name
Your Address
Your City, State ZIP

Date

Creditor Name
Creditor Address
Creditor City, State ZIP

RE: **[insert name on account]**
        Account # **[insert account number]**

To Whom It May Concern:

In reviewing my credit report, I noticed the following discrepancy reported by your company regarding the account listed above:

[Insert relevant information and explanation of error. *Example:*

> ***ABC Bank, Account # 123456***
> ***Current balance on credit report is $1,500.00***
> ***My records show this balance paid in full as of February 17, 2005.]***

I requested a reinvestigation through **[insert name of Credit Bureau]** and was informed that the information listed is correct. I have enclosed copies of **[insert names of Documents]** which show the error.

Please review this matter, correct this discrepancy, and contact me in writing within 30 days to verify that you have complied with this request.

Thank you for your assistance.

Sincerely,

[sign your name here]

Your Name
SSN and DOB

Letter to Request Accounts be Added to Your Credit Report

Your Name
Your Address
Your City, State Zip

Date

Creditor Name
Creditor Address
Creditor City, State Zip

RE: Acct #: **[insert account #]**
      Name: **[insert your name]**
      Address: **[insert your current address]**
      Social Security Number: **[insert your SSN]**
      Date of Birth: **[insert your DOB]**

To Whom It May Concern:

While reviewing my credit report from **[insert name of bureau(s) not showing tradeline]**, I realized there were account(s) not being reported by your company. I understand that you are not required by law to report these items, but I respectfully request that you contact **[insert name of bureau(s)]** and have the tradeline(s) listed below added to my credit file:

[insert your account#(s)]

Please respond to this letter in writing within 30 days verifying that the update has been sent, or giving an explanation from your company confirming that you don't report to **[enter bureau(s) name]**.

Thank you for your assistance.

Sincerely,

[sign your name here]

Your Name

Letter to Request a 100-Word Statement be Added to Your Credit Report

Your Name
Your Address
Your City, State Zip

Date

Credit Bureau Name
Credit Bureau Address
Credit Bureau City, State Zip

RE: Credit File of **[insert your name]**
        SSN **[insert your SSN]**

To Whom It May Concern:

Under section 611(b) of the Fair Credit Reporting Act, I am requesting that the following consumer statement be inserted into my credit report exactly as follows: **[insert your 100 word statement]**

For example only:

> *From April 2004 to October 2004, I was out of work due to illness and was unable to meet all my financial obligations. After prioritizing my expenses, I was forced to pay less than the required amount to my unsecured creditors. When I returned to work, I made arrangements with the creditors, became current, and continued to pay my obligations. Thank you for your understanding.*

Please send me an updated copy of my credit report once the above statement has been added to my credit file. Thank you very much.

Sincerely,

[sign your name here]

Your Name

Dispute and Debt Validation Request for Dunning Letter

Your Name
Your Address
Your City, State Zip

Date

Debt Collector Name
Debt Collector Address
Debt Collector City, State Zip

Re: VERIFICATION AND VALIDATION of Acct # **[insert acct #]**

To Whom It May Concern:

This letter is in response to the letter I received from you on **[insert date]**; a copy of which is attached herein. This is not a refusal to pay, but a notice sent pursuant to the Fair Debt Collection Practices Act, 15 USC 1692g Sec. 809 (b) that your claim is hereby disputed and validation is requested.

Please provide me with the following showing that I have a legal obligation to pay you:

1. Identity of the original creditor
2. An explanation of how the balance of the alleged debt was calculated
3. A copy of any agreement between you and the original creditor showing you are legally entitled to collect monies on this account
4. A verification or copy of any judgment, if applicable
5. Proof that the Statute of Limitations has not expired on this account
6. Proof that you are licensed to collect in my state

Failure to comply fully and completely with the above validation requests before continuing collection attempts, or reporting this account to any consumer reporting agency, is a violation of Federal law and will result in complaints being filed with the Federal Trade Commission, my state Attorney General's office and your state Attorney General's office. Civil and criminal claims may also be pursued.

Sincerely,

[sign your name here]

Your Name

Dispute and Debt Validation Request for 30+ Days After Dunning Letter

Your Name
Your Address
Your City, State Zip

Date

Debt Collector Name
Debt Collector Address
Debt Collector City, State Zip

Re: VERIFICATION AND VALIDATION of Acct # **[insert acct #]**

To Whom It May Concern:

[Choose paragraph 1 *or* 2 *or* write one that fits your situation.]

1. In reviewing my credit file I noticed that you are reporting an account that I have no knowledge of and for which I NEVER RECEIVED A NOTICE OF DEBT from your company as required by the Fair Debt Collection Practices Act, 15 USC 1692g Sec. 809 (a).

[OR]

2. Today I received a collection notice from you on **[insert date]**; a copy of which is attached herein. I have no knowledge of and NEVER RECEIVED A NOTICE OF DEBT from your company as required by the Fair Debt Collection Practices Act, 15 USC 1692g Sec. 809 (a).

I am willing to excuse this violation as an oversight on your part, yet now that I am aware of this alleged debt, I am exercising my rights under the Fair Debt Collection Practices Act, 15 USC 1692g Sec. 809 (b) and put you on notice that your claim is hereby disputed and validation is requested.

Please provide me with the following showing that I have a legal obligation to pay you:

1. Identity of the original creditor
2. An explanation of how the balance of the alleged debt was calculated
3. A copy of any agreement between you and the original creditor showing you are legally entitled to collect monies on this account
4. A verification or copy of any judgment, if applicable
5. Proof that the Statute of Limitations has not expired on this account
6. Proof that you are licensed to collect in my state

Failure to comply fully and completely with the above validation requests before continuing collection attempts, or reporting this account to any consumer reporting agency, is a violation of Federal law and will result in complaints being filed with the Federal Trade Commission, my state Attorney General's office and your state Attorney General's office. Civil and criminal claims may also be pursued.

Sincerely,

[sign your name here]

Your Name

Call Log

Date: _____ Time of Call: _____

Place of Call: _____

Name of Company: _____

Caller's Name: _____

Caller's Phone #: _____

Notes/Comments: (Describe the conversation, especially any FDCPA violations)

_____

_____

_____

_____

_____

_____

_____

_____

Do Not Call Letter

Your Name
Your Address
Your City, State Zip

Date

Creditor Name
Creditor Address
Creditor City, State Zip

To Whom It May Concern:

I am writing to demand that you cease telephone communications with me according to section [15 USC 1692c] §805(c) of the Fair Debt Collection Practices Act (FDCPA).

Stop calling me at home, at work, on my cell phone, or at any other location!

In accordance with the FDCPA, now that you have received this "stop calling" letter, you may only contact me to inform me that you:

- Are terminating further collection efforts
- Might invoke a specified remedy
- Intend to invoke a specified remedy

Since you obviously already have my contact information, calls also made by you or your company to any third party concerning me is in violation of section [15 USC 1692c] §805(b) of the FDCPA.

Be advised that I am keeping accurate records of all correspondence from you and your company, including phone calls. If you continue calling me I will file complaints with the Federal Trade Commission and your state Attorney General and sue you for FDCPA violations.

Signature

[sign your name here]

Your Name

Notification of a Time-Barred Debt

Your Name
Your Address
Your City, State Zip

Date

Creditor Name
Creditor Address
Creditor City, State Zip

RE: Account # **[insert account number here]**

To Whom It May Concern:

This letter is to inform you that the above referenced account is now a **time-barred debt** according to **[insert your state's legal code reference; e.g., RCW 4.16.040 of Washington State]** and is no longer collectable.

This notice is also a demand that you **cease all communications** with me according to section [15 USC 1692c] §805(c) of the Fair Debt Collection Practices Act (FDCPA).

Any further contact or collection attempts will result in legal action against your company.

Signature

[sign your name here]

Your Name

Settlement Agreement

THIS AGREEMENT ON DISPUTED ACCOUNT (hereinafter "Agreement"), is made and effective as of **[insert date of agreement]** [the "Effective Date"] by and between **Acme Collections, a California corporation** with its principal offices located at **123 Collections Lane, Los Angeles, CA 12345** (hereinafter "Creditor"), and **[insert your name]** (hereinafter "Debtor"), residing at **[insert your address]**.

WHEREAS Creditor asserts to hold certain claims against Debtor for **[enter account information]** in the amount of **[enter amount allegedly owed]**;

AND WHEREAS Debtor disputes said claim and denies said debt is due; AND WHEREAS parties desire to resolve and forever settle said claim.

NOW, THEREFORE, Debtor agrees to pay to Creditor and Creditor agrees to accept from Debtor simultaneously herewith, the sum of **[settlement amount]** in full payment, settlement, satisfaction, discharge, and release of said claim and in release of any further claims thereto.

Creditor acknowledges that if any adverse report(s) has been filed by Creditor with any credit bureau regarding this disputed account, it/they will be removed immediately **[or updated to "paid as agreed" if applicable]** upon receipt of the settlement funds. Creditor further agrees to never reinsert any information relative to this account on Debtor's credit reports.

This agreement shall be binding upon and inure to the benefit of all the parties, their successors, assigns and personal representatives.

IN WITNESS WHEREOF the parties hereto have executed this Agreement as of the date first written above.

CREDITOR   **DEBTOR**

_____   _____
Authorized Signature   Authorized Signature

_____   _____
Printed Name   Printed Name

_____
Title

Limited Money Back Guarantee

DebtClear is so confident in its educational materials that it will provide those who purchase The DebtClear Roadmap: A Comprehensive Guide to Debt Relief, Credit Repair, Asset Protection and Creditor Lawsuits a 500% limited money back guarantee subject to the following terms and limitations.

If you follow the DebtClear methods identified in The DebtClear Roadmap: A Comprehensive Guide to Debt Relief, Credit Repair, Asset Protection and Creditor Lawsuits from start to finish, we guarantee that you will pay less than twenty (20) cents on the dollar to settle your qualifying unsecured debt or we will refund 500% of the purchase price of the book. To be eligible for this refund, you must demonstrate that you followed the DebtClear methods identified in The DebtClear Roadmap: A Comprehensive Guide to Debt Relief, Credit Repair, Asset Protection and Creditor Lawsuits from start to finish by meeting ALL of the following requirements:

1. All of your unsecured debts must be no less than 90 days in default and still with the original creditor at the time of purchase;
2. You must provide us with copies of the credit reports you obtained by you within seven (7) business days of purchasing your book from all three (3) major credit reporting agencies;
3. You must provide us with a copies of your current credit reports from all three (3) major credit reporting agencies obtained by you within thirty (30) days of making your claim against this money back guarantee;
4. You must respond to all initial debt collection letters (or their verbal equivalent) within 30 days with a request for verification and validation of the alleged debt amount and a statement of dispute as to the outstanding balance identified, if such dispute is accurate. You must provide us with copies of these initial debt collection letters and

copies of your timely letters in response, including copies of certified mailing and return receipts.

5. You must provide us with proof of maintaining a creditor call log.
6. You must provide us with proof that no unsecured debts have been settled before a lawsuit has been filed by your unsecured creditor(s) seeking collection of such debt before settlement;
7. You must provide us with a copy of any lawsuit(s) filed against you by your unsecured creditor(s);
8. The statue of limitations must have expired on the unsecured debt you are claiming against this limited money back guarantee;
9. You must provide us with a copy of your purchase receipt.

Send all documents to the mailing address shown at www.debtclear.com/about-us.

9 781450 776462